Dave Carley
Three Plays

3 PLAYS BY
Dave Carley

Writing With Our Feet
Midnight Madness
Into

Dave Carley: Three Plays
first published 2003 by
Scirocco Drama
An imprint of J. Gordon Shillingford Publishing Inc.
© 2003 Dave Carley

Into was originally published by Playwrights Canada Press (1993), *Midnight Madness*
by Summerhill Press (1989) and *Writing With Our Feet* by Blizzard Publishing (1992).

Scirocco Drama Series Editor: Glenda MacFarlane
Cover Design by Doowah Design Inc.
Cover photo by Nir Bareket
Author photo by Michael Lee
Printed and bound in Canada

We acknowledge the financial assistance of The Canada Council for the Arts
and the Manitoba Arts Council for our publishing program.

Production inquiries should be addressed to:
Patricia Ney, Christopher Banks and Associates
6 Adelaide Street, Suite 610
Toronto, Ontario, Canada M5C 1H6
416-214-1155
cbanks@pathcom.com

Canadian Cataloguing in Publication Data

Carley, Dave, 1955–
        Dave Carley: three plays.

Contents: into—Midnight madness—Writing with our feet.
ISBN 0-920486-43-6

I. Title. II. Title: Thhree plays. III. Title: Into. IV. Title: Midnight
madness. V. Title: Writing with our feet.

PS8555.A7397D39 2003   C812'.54   C2003-903949-8

J. Gordon Shillingford Publishing
P.O. Box 86, RPO Corydon Avenue, Winnipeg, MB Canada R3M 3S3

Contents

Dave Carley

Dave Carley is one Canada's most produced playwrights. In addition to the three plays collected in this volume, he has written *Walking on Water*, *After You* and *Taking Liberties*. He has adapted a novel by Margaret Atwood (*The Edible Woman*), a collection of stories by Helen Weinzweig (*A View From the Roof*), and written a number of radio plays which have been broadcast nationally on CBC. His journalism has appeared in a variety of publications, ranging from *Time* magazine to *The Kawartha Sun*. He was founding editor of *CanPlay*, the Playwright Guild of Canada's magazine, and has also edited two anthologies of radio plays, *Take Five* and *AirPlay*. In 2000, Dave received the Arthur Miller Playwriting Award from the University of Michigan and he has won a number of other national and international awards for his writing. Dave lives in Toronto. His website is www.davecarley.com

Foreword

Although they're not much more than a decade old, *Midnight Madness*, *Writing With Our Feet* and *Into* bring to mind a career's-worth of actors, directors and designers. These plays have been performed in a variety of theatres, to audiences happy and not so happy. I have been brave at their opening nights, occasionally fearful and/or medicated, and once I met the mayor of Hamilton while cowering under a table. I cut my theatrical teeth on these plays and they made my choice of profession irrevocable.

Midnight Madness, *Writing With Our Feet* and *Into* were written in reasonably rapid succession, between 1987 and 1993. In addition to their chronological proximity, they have other links. They are comedies. All three plays are concerned with personal change and growth within, or in opposition to, the context of a wider community. I have written other more overtly political plays; they are (as one might expect) less popular though perhaps more cathartic to write. I have also adapted the works of other writers—most notably Helen Weinzweig and Margaret Atwood—and that has brought a great deal of (very different, slightly vicarious) creative pleasure. But, although *Into* is "inspired" by a Julio Cortazar story, *Midnight Madness*, *Writing With Our Feet* and *Into* are all very much originals; I take full and sole responsibility for them.

The plays in this collection have also been widely performed, from Perth, Australia to Yellowknife, Northwest Territories, in most Canadian provinces and in many American theatres. I like to think they are popular for the right reasons—as good pieces of theatre that connect with their audiences. I don't write to satisfy myself; that just isn't going to happen. Any gratification I get from this process has to come from the effect these plays have on others; to have them produced so widely has, of itself, been my reward.

One other thing that links these collected trio: I have rewritten the damn things a dozen times each. I must have been a plastic surgeon in a previous life, or a serial alchemist. I cannot seem to leave my plays alone, and the great advantage of having so many productions is that I've had unlimited opportunities to fine-tune them. Most of the rewriting has been just that—tinkering—but in some cases entire characters and scenes have vanished into the ether. The plays are generally better for the surgery, but there does come a time when a playwright has to let go, and—to paraphrase the last line of *Writing With Our Feet*— "Now is most definitely the time".

  So here they are. I've been asked to spin a few words on them, and to do that I should begin by describing a funeral I attended long ago, in my formative years. An elderly relation had died; a good woman who had lived a good life in a good, small town. Our family congregated outside the church before the service. (In those days, in those towns, as a sign of respect the grieving kin of the deceased would enter the church en masse and take up the front pews. I would later know this as 'making an entrance'). Just before we were given our cue to enter, an errant uncle let fly with an especially funny and incorrect joke that had to do with the deceased's physical handicap. Our entire family dissolved into wild and guilty giggles on the church step, then sucked it up and trooped in. But throughout the service I could see familial shoulders quaking, and I knew that some of the tears that day were not ones of sorrow. It was a very good joke.

  I still think about that funeral. Although this is likely a truth I was already inhaling from a family addicted to gallows laughter, it was precisely summed up for me that day: you can't have the serious without the ludicrous. This entire journey of life is pretty foolish, and there's no reason to treat its finish any differently. And that also applies to the little journeys we take whenever the lights go down in a theatre. No matter how serious it is, life pounds the boards with the ridiculous—or it just isn't real.

  So I call these three plays comedies and I can maybe even break that down further: *Midnight Madness* is a gentle one, *Writing With Our Feet* veers into blackness; and *Into* is a bit surreal. Apart from the humour, and some thematic links, the plays are very different stylistically. I began my playwriting career mired—and I use that term willingly—in naturalism. I came from a time, place and era where the only theatre I could see was naturalistic and, never having had an academic background in the profession, I had no way of being aware that there were other writing options. I also had no idea how restrictive naturalism is, how claustrophobic, how unnecessary it is (or how popular it is with audiences) until I wrote *Midnight Madness*. I wouldn't begin to break free until I began *Writing With Our Feet* and, for the most part and to varying degrees, I have been dramatic off-roading ever since. I suppose I shouldn't slag naturalism, in that it has served me well and put bread on my table. *Midnight Madness* is an hour and a half of real-time in the life of a bed salesman, and those ninety minutes have been seen in forty to fifty productions coast to coast. The play, written in 1987-88 (and, of course, revised ever since), was my second Equity-produced play, following on the heels of *Sister Jude*. That play was a flawed piece that focused on Wesley Marshall, a young man with a keen sense of personal sin and concomitant thirst for salvation. The story that formed its spine won the *Toronto Star* Short Story Contest and ever-economic, I had grown it into a full-length play. Structurally *Sister Jude* was all over the place; somehow I figured that out, and I set out to rectify that with my new play. As a result, *Midnight Madness* was carefully and logically plotted. It also featured poor Wesley again—as he aged, there became more sins to enumerate, more salvation to bestow.

By the time *Midnight Madness* takes place, Wesley is employed selling beds—the catalysts of other people's pleasure but certainly not of his. He works upstairs in a dying furniture store on a main street that is gasping for its economic life. Wesley bears scrapbook witness to the evolving lives of his old classmates, while fighting hard to live as little and as obscurely as possible. Central to this is his ability to fly low under the sexual radar. So it seems only natural that, in the last moments of his store's history, Anna Bregner, an old classmate, fellow pariah and Woman With A Past should bound up the steps to his Bed Department.

The leap of faith that often fires our major life decisions fascinates me. I tend to think it is most often a cumulative thing, but occasionally there can be a dramatic snap of will, and that of course makes for better theatre. Wesley (and later, Jean-François) will make big personal leaps, but not before they get a lot of pushing and, in Wesley's case, that's about ninety minutes' worth. He was an awfully easy person to write because I share some of his characteristics, as do we all. In *Into*, Lucy Cormier says, "Comfort is false" but for anyone prone to hibernation, it is also a necessity.

I was still close enough to my high school years that I could also remember and write about the horrible cruelties that abounded there, especially as they were visited upon the weak, meek and square. I suspect that this is the key to the enduring resonance of *Midnight Madness*—everyone in every audience has been the brunt of some awful deed or insult in high school and, if they weren't the brunt, they were by definition the brunt-givers. Quite often they were both. And so within the walls of a gentle naturalistic play I'm offering up a highball of remembered guilt with a chaser of expiation.

The other thing I wanted to address in *Midnight Madness* was the death of the small town downtown and, in particular, local control over our economic destiny. A wonderful and perhaps even romantic period in our retail history was drawing to a close in the 1980s. The chain stores were taking over from the independents, the malls began spreading like retail melanoma (and the big boxes hovered in the wings—or suburbs). Our eclectic and vital downtowns withered. In my hometown of Peterborough (which I thinly disguise as "Ashburnham") many of the old stores were owned by Jewish families, who lived and prospered in a tiny counterpoint to the overwhelming WASPness of the city. And in many small cities these small but viable communities have dwindled along with their stores. I wanted to position Wesley against this backdrop—the end of Bloom's Furniture was looming over this head; his way of life was ending just as certainly as that of his eighty year-old employer and his particular little subset of Upper Canadian society. The play is a lament for the passing of those great family stores; they and their owners had a personality (and a commitment to their street and community) that no mall or big box will ever possess.

Midnight Madness was initially co-produced with the Muskoka Festival in Gravenhurst, Peterborough's Arbor Theatre and Toronto's Tarragon. Bill Glassco directed the play's development and premiere production. Bill is truly a gentle/man and the play was informed with his respectful touch. He perceived *Midnight Madness* as a character study and we concentrated on that, with the help of two gifted actors, Michelle Fisk and John Dolan. (In an early victory for non-traditional casting, Graham Greene played the offstage voice of Mr. Bloom). It became clear that in order for the play to work—because it isn't exactly rife with dramatic action—it was necessary for the actors to completely inhabit their characters, and my job was to make that possible.

That production bestowed a rare, early gift on my career. As *Midnight Madness* travelled from Gravenhurst to Peterborough and then to Toronto, I had an opportunity to do a huge amount of rewriting. And to *learn* how to rewrite. In the subsequent decade and a half, its continued popularity has allowed me to tinker to my heart's content. (Oddly, unlike both *Into* and *Writing With Our Feet*, *Midnight Madness* has never been produced in the United States. Perhaps Wesley is simply too repressed for our American cousins. On the other hand, Wesley does set out to remake himself—both at the YMCA and then outside his furniture department—and surely that locks into the American Dream?)

Wesley and Anna reappear in *Two Ships Passing* (written ten years after *Midnight Madness*.) As you might be suspecting, I have a terrible time letting go of my characters. They are family and, if I can't rewrite them, then I want to reintroduce them. And knowing how much my own life has changed over the past decade, it seems almost unfair to leave them frozen in time. And so, in *Two Ships Passing*, Wesley discovers his libido, and the left-leaning Anna becomes an activist judge. Anna's son Jason—a pre-teen in *Midnight Madness*—is now a right-wing apologist of the *National Post* ilk. The offstage Mr. Bloom is dead (golfing, Florida) but I did bring him back centre stage in a later play, *Walking on Water*, where we discover the early source of his business success. And Bloom's son Ron appears in two other more political plays, *Taking Liberties* and *The Last Liberal*.

At first glance, *Writing With Our Feet* seems a great departure from *Midnight Madness*. Stylistically that is true, but thematically it's not. Written largely in 1989-90, it continues with many of the themes first explored in *Midnight Madness*. The central character, Jean-François, is agoraphobic; he lives in a garage and must gird his loins to leave. In this case, there is an existing, peripheral love interest in JF's life but the main force for positive change is his sister, Sophie. She hovers over his foot garage, summoning up a bizarre cavalcade of would-be JF-outers.

The writing process for *Writing With Our Feet* was entirely different. Whereas I had carefully plotted Midnight Madness, this play was an exercise in automatic writing. It happened in two spurts—first the initial narrative scene (which was performed as a short piece at Alberta Theatre Projects' Brave New Works) and then the full play. If I added up the total writing time for the first draft, it could not have been more than three or four days. It just flew out. I can't explain it. I didn't realize in advance that JF and Co.—

superficially so unlike me and my world—were in residence, but there they were and here they are. Not everyone was amused. The play was nominated for the 1992 Governor General's Award and in those days *The Globe and Mail* hired a fusty University of Toronto professor to conduct an annual excoriation of the nominees. The play was beyond the poor man's ken, but he did manage to bray about appropriation of voice, as he claimed I was not of JF's ethnic background. (I'm assuming he spent a few days researching the various ins and outs of my family tree.)

I have never known of anyone who is genuinely creative raise the appropriation issue. Those of us who are actually "doing it" spend our lives engaged in a thousand acts of appropriation, and it is *that* ability that needs be judged. In this collection of three plays I have—among others—appropriated the voice of a Roman Catholic priest (I'm most definitely neither); a dead car designer (I'm alive and writing plays); a legless drunkard (I still have my legs), and a disaffected white youth (one out of three). That said, some of *Writing With Our Feet* has also grown from personal experience, including the central metaphor. As I state in the play's dedication, my sister and I really did learn how to write with our feet, out of fear that we might one day lose the use of our hands. *Writing With Our Feet* is about a pair of odd siblings and I'm not sure it gets much stranger than two kids spending time developing a legible toe-script.

With *Writing With Our Feet* I also learned that when a play arrives unbidden there's always a danger—or benefit—that characters may also appear who at first blush don't fit. In *Midnight Madness*, there's a clear logic to who appears in that dusty bed department, but the rules break down in *Writing With Our Feet*. Raymond Loewy—the celebrated designer who was justly named by *Time* magazine as one of the 100 most influential people of the 20th century—has no business lurking in JF's Montreal garage. But Loewy haunts me, so there he is. I've long admired Loewy's work— beginning with another (odd) childhood fixation, this one with Studebakers. As I learned more about Loewy, I began to realize his seminal impact on how we live our lives. Loewy fervently believed that good design should not be hidden behind museum walls or in the salons of the rich—it should exist in our everyday life. It could be as simple as the curvaceous utility of a Coca Cola bottle or as visual arresting as a bullet-nosed Studebaker. Loewy wanted to fill his adopted America with functional beauty—art that worked. JF—

if he is to be a true disciple of Loewy—must also take his foot-creations to the public.

Some of the other characters were surprises too. I have an aunt who has publicly claimed to be the model for battle-axe Aunt Zenaïde, but in truth she's far too well-behaved. Aunt Zenaïde just "sprang". And, although other relatives have sex lives that would make the peccadilloes of Alphonsinette fairly pale by comparison, I have not yet portrayed their excesses. With the exception of Loewy and the idea that two children might actually spend time foot-writing, *Writing With Our Feet* is utterly fictional, appropriated from the murkier recesses of my brain.

Like *Midnight Madness*, the play is about community and the courage needed to participate fully in it. Again, it loops back to my own populist instincts; like Loewy, I cannot see any use in creating if it is not taken outside the garage. That great Canadian play curse that George F. Walker calls "The Dixie Cup Syndrome" hangs over me like a cautionary sword; I don't want my plays to be produced once and then tossed to the side of the cultural thruway. I want them to be done and done, and done. Naturally, that cannot dictate or even shape the writing process but, ultimately, process is process, and only process. The real payoff in this trade comes when those theatre lights dim.

Luckily, *Writing With Our Feet* has also had a great number of productions across North America and I've again used that opportunity to do some fine-tuning. The first production, by Theatre Terra Nova, took place in a one-time Hamilton porn palace that that fledgling company was renovating. *Writing With Our Feet* was the opening play in its musty new space. The company decided to throw open the theatre's doors for the official premiere, in order to thank the residents of the city—it was, after all, their tax dollars that was funding the restoration. Back then, *Writing With Our Feet* clocked in at well over two hours. After the mayor cut the ribbon and the lights went down, things got harrowing. The audience was expecting a light comedy and, indeed, some of the more traditional patrons were expecting some heavy porn. I was giving them overlong, surrealistic mayhem. I retreated at intermission to the theatre office and somehow found myself under a table. I cannot remember exactly how or why I went under that table. I do remember the office door opening during the second act and a very tall man (they are all tall when you're hiding under a table) entered to use the phone. He noticed me with not a great deal of surprise—apparently under-tabled men are commonplace in Hamilton—and asked me what I was doing there. "I wrote the play," I replied. Mayor Morrow shrugged and went about his civic duties.

Luckily the play's life did not end there. A Toronto premiere directed by Jackie Maxwell followed, first with Stephen Ouimette and Tanja Jacobs, and then with Tom McCamus and Ellie Rae Hennessey in a remount a year later. As with the triple production of *Midnight Madness* this gave me the chance I needed to hone the play into proper shape. That extra half hour was shaved and I remained free-standing at both Factory opening nights.

The new set of lessons I learned from *Writing With Our Feet* have served me well. First, I realized—the Hamilton opening night fiasco notwithstanding—that audiences are ever-willing to take risks and are actually pretty patient. (The Hamilton premiere still got a standing ovation but maybe they just needed to stretch their legs.) I realized, if I didn't know it already, that there were strengths inherent in theatre that weren't present elsewhere. Primary among those opportunities was the elasticity you have with time and place. Theatre audiences are very quick to embrace non-naturalism and I decided it would be a shame to ever again waste that chance.

At some point over the intervening years after *Midnight Madness* and *Writing With Our Feet* I seem to have developed a more benign view of community and the possibilities it offers society's marginals. The community in Wesley's case is stifling, judgmental, and in *Writing With Our Feet* it is a scary, external force. But in *Into* a viable community is necessary for both survival and nurture. And it works best when it is diverse—whereas Wesley and Anna were suppressed by a moral monolith, *Into* features four disparate personalities forced together. And fractious though their little unit is, it affords greater potential for happiness than the adjacent, homogenous groupings: the novacain-addicted Dental Confederation or the angry Anne Murrayites and, worst of all, the Disaffected Youth with their bad music and incessant brawling. Different is good, and even better when it stands united.

Into was inspired by the Julio Cortazar story "The Southern Thruway". My involvement began by adapting the Argentinian's short story for a radio drama, as part of a Cortazar series that producer Bill Lane had commissioned at CBC. The radio version stuck closely to Cortazar's text, the story of a traffic jam that lasts for hours and longer, and featured a male narrator. The radio version was about twenty-five minutes long.

Next stop was the Toronto Fringe Festival, where I so radically changed the story and characters that I decided the proper attribution for Cortazar's influence was "inspired" rather than calling it an adaptation. The characters were all changed, the highway moved to North America, I placed a nun stage centre and began the play with a long monologue. All I retained was the basic premise of the story—a traffic jam and the fragile community it created.

Amid all this magic realism, I also injected some straight-ahead storytelling. The nun's monologue at the top of the play was my chosen way of venting my anger at the Catholic church for its increasingly reactionary positions on any number of social issues. What should be, and periodically is, a liberating institution for social progress was being dragged relentlessly back into the dark ages by the Pope and, locally, a pair of reactionary Cardinals. As Boy says in the play, "It really made me mad." I sharpened my metaphorical buns and began tossing them. I was told constantly that giving over the first fifteen minutes of a play to a monologue, before going into a more conventional structure, "just wouldn't work", that you couldn't have two stylistically dissimilar sections in a play without somehow alienating the audience. I thank God I didn't listen because the nun's monologue has always worked. (I've noticed that the two biggest under-estimators of audience intelligence are theatre programmers and theatre professionals.)

The Fringe show was a hit and I expanded it yet again for stage, this time a 90 minute version at Theatre Passe Muraille. Bill Lane—the original radio producer—came and directed the Dora-nominated show and most of the cast returned from the Fringe version. *Into* has been subsequently been performed from Perth, Australia to Yellowknife, Northwest Territories, to Halifax, proving I guess that there is indeed a universality to our need for community or, failing that, traffic jams.

My work is of no consequence if it is not performed, but it is surely a wonderful thing to have it collected on paper. As these plays now go to print, I vow that there will be no more rewrites. Luckily, the rewriting impulse eventually yields to the drive to create something new. That ginger step out of the bed department or foot garage is part of a writer's daily routine, or should be. But as I eject this disk, I find myself exceptionally grateful that these plays are being preserved in this volume. They are a big part of my life and it would be unnatural for me not to hope that they can't be a small part of yours.

Dave Carley
Toronto, 2003

Midnight Madness

for Bill Glassco

Acknowledgments

The creation of *Midnight Madness* was generously assisted by the Ontario Arts Council. A workshop was conducted at the Muskoka Festival in the summer of 1987, directed by Bill Glassco, with John Dolan as Wesley and Michelle Fisk as Anna. The author would like to thank Bill Glassco, John Dolan and Michelle Fisk; and also Michael Ayoub, Jennifer Dean, Graham Greene, Glenda MacFarlane, Chris McHarge, Kevin McGugan, Patricia Ney, Judith Rudakoff, Michael Shamata, Myles Warren and Helen Weinzweig.

Production Information

Midnight Madness premiered on August 11, 1988, at the Gravenhurst Opera House, Gravenhurst, Ontario, as a co-production of the Muskoka Festival, Arbor and Tarragon theatres. The cast was as follows:

WESLEY: John Dolan
ANNA: Michelle Fisk
MR. BLOOM: Graham Greene

Director: Bill Glassco
Assistant Director: Michael Shamata
Set and Costume Design: Myles Warren
Lighting Design: Andrew Rabbets
Sound Design: Evan B. Turner

The play was restaged by Michael Shamata with the same cast, and opened at Toronto's Tarragon Theatre on October 18, 1988.

Characters

WESLEY Marshall, about 32
ANNA Bregner, the same age
The voice of Mr. BLOOM, 75

Setting

The second-floor Bed Department of Bloom's Furniture, a rundown store on the main street of Ashburnham (Ash-burn-m), a small city in Ontario.

Offstage is the Lighting Department, identifiable by a glow. Everything in the Bed Department is marked down, including a cannonball bed, a fairly rococo brass number and a large waterbed unit. There is some terrible velvet-type art on the walls—large seascapes and stags in mountain glens.

The time is 1985.

Note: Mr. Bloom does NOT speak with a heavy Jewish accent. Such an accent is completely implausible for a man who has lived his entire life in a small Ontario city.

Midnight Madness

Act One

The play begins in darkness. BLOOM's voice is heard over the intercom speaker.

BLOOM: Wesley. Try again.

WESLEY: OK, how's this: "One old Jew. One young Presbyterian. Two men, a hundred and eight years of accumulated guilt."

BLOOM: I don't like that word guilt. It makes me nervous.

WESLEY: But wait—I'm going to tie it in with selling the bed. "These men understand sin. They know all about crimes of passion. They can sell you the weapon –

Lights up. WESLEY is on the waterbed, holding the intercom mike in one hand and a styrofoam cup of sherry in the other.

The revolutionary Waterbed Home Entertainment Centre, complete with stereo headboard, climate control and the Undulation Feature. Motion below to match the motion above. Friends, customers: come to Bloom's and invest in some liquid guilt."

BLOOM: *(Enjoying himself.)* Too racy. And the religious stuff still makes me nervous. But it shows promise. You should go into advertising after tomorrow.

WESLEY: Yeah, yeah.

BLOOM: You know hundreds of fancy words; you could sell all sorts of things.

WESLEY: I haven't unloaded this waterbed yet, have I. And we've only got one day left. Jeez sir—I haven't had a customer in an hour.

BLOOM: You think it's a mob scene down here?

WESLEY: This Midnight Madness idea—I don't know. It just isn't the hour for buying furniture. This is the hour of marital duty.

BLOOM: It's nearly midnight! They got that done by nine-thirty. Think of some more funny ads.

WESLEY: Why don't we close for the night?

BLOOM: The sign says we're open to midnight, so we stay open. Do that Marxist one again. I liked it. "Rise up couch potatoes of the world." Come on, humour an old man.

WESLEY: I'm gonna miss this place.

BLOOM: No mush, my son.

WESLEY: This isn't mush, this is reality. I've got pre-partum depression.

BLOOM: You should talk normal, you could get a girl. And save the emotion for tomorrow. Mrs. B's making us a cake, I've got some nice wine, we'll drink this store out in style. Tomorrow. But it's still today, we've got time on our hands and, if you don't want to make up ads, you should go dust.

WESLEY: *(With him.)* Dust.

BLOOM: If the legs worked better I'd be up there in a flash and I bet if I ran my finger down the headboard of your precious stereo waterbed I'd find—dust.

WESLEY: *(Rubbing his sleeve over the headboard.)* Clean as a baby's bum.

BLOOM: Fifty years, I've never had an employee who

dusted. Not a one. *(Pause.)* For heaven's sake, there's someone coming in the door! Customer alert! *(Voice fading as he approaches the customer; intercom was left on.)* Hello, young lady.

ANNA: Hi.

BLOOM: Lovely evening isn't it. What can I do you for?

ANNA: Is the Bed Department still upstairs?

BLOOM: Oh yes, it's this way—the stairs are behind the clocks there. Watch the last step dear. *(Over intercom.)* Snap to it Wes, maybe you can unload the waterbed!

WESLEY has leapt into action, dusting a headboard or two, straightening a bedspread, adjusting his tie. It's a fairly co-ordinated, practised sequence, which he completes by flipping on the muzak. ANNA enters, frowning back at the step. She sees WESLEY and smiles.

WESLEY: Hi. May I help you?

ANNA: You could start by fixing that step. I nearly killed myself.

WESLEY: It's even worse going down.

ANNA: A little gnome told me the beds were here.

WESLEY: And did he tell you everything's on sale?

ANNA: I saw the ad in *The Examiner*.

WESLEY: Cash or cheque. Coloured beads. Wampum. Just no credit. *(Pause.)* I know you.

ANNA: Those are the three scariest words in the language.

WESLEY: We went to Ashburnham High together.

ANNA: Stinky Harrison!

WESLEY: No.

ANNA: Baldy McLaren?

WESLEY: Wesley Marshall.

ANNA: Wesley Marshall—Jude's brother! You've changed!

WESLEY: I'm less blemished. You're Anna Bregner.

ANNA: I'm flattered you recognize me.

WESLEY: You haven't changed a bit, hardly.

ANNA: Wesley Marshall.

WESLEY: Yeah.

ANNA: I haven't seen you since high school. How many years is that –

WESLEY: Fourteen.

ANNA: God. Your sister and I were best friends for— weeks. We did everything together, then she stole Billy Dingle from me.

WESLEY: They got married.

ANNA: Yeah, I heard. Well, isn't this something! What're you doing here, anyway.

WESLEY: I'm second floor manager. For one more day. Then we're retail history.

ANNA: I can't imagine downtown without Bloom's. *(Points to cannonball bed.)* The cannonball's nice.

WESLEY: Solid pine.

ANNA: Made in Canada?

WESLEY: Nah. *(Brightening.)* It might be assembled here, though. I betcha the wood's ours.

BLOOM:	*(Intercom.)* Welcome to Bloom's Midnight Madness Sale. For the next ten minutes everything is 10 percent off the last 25 percent off. Especially beds and lighting.
ANNA:	Is that Bloom?
WESLEY:	Yup.
ANNA:	He's cute.
WESLEY:	Cute!?
ANNA:	Sweet.
WESLEY:	Bloom! He's grumpy, nosey, bossy...
ANNA:	I don't believe you.
WESLEY:	Believe me.
ANNA:	How long have you worked for him, then?
WESLEY:	Just a decade. Started in the Spring of '75.
ANNA:	Ten years!
WESLEY:	Why not? I'm fond of the old guy.
ANNA:	Apparently. *(Of the muzak.)* And you've listened to that muzak the whole time?
WESLEY:	Awful eh. Just a sec and I'll put on something better.
	He turns off the muzak, mucks about for cassette tapes.
ANNA:	*(Of the brass bed.)* These things always remind me of Bob Dylan.
WESLEY:	*(Off a bit.)* You want some Bob Dylan?
ANNA:	No, I said this bed reminds me of him. "Lay lady lay..."

WESLEY: I thought you wanted Dylan. I haven't got much new stuff. Post-1900. Hey—do you remember Miss Eaton's English class, how she'd pull apart the lyrics of songs? She always said it should be "Lie Lady, Lie."

ANNA: Miss Eaton reminded me of a chipping sparrow on acid.

WESLEY: I never thought of her that way, but you're right. And that other song, with the line, "Ain't no one for to give you no pain." Triple negative, it used to drive her around the bend. Billy'd whistle it at the back. *(Distracted from putting on tape.)* You were front corner by the door. Till Christmas—

ANNA: You have quite the memory. So tell me, why should I buy a brass bed?

WESLEY: Beats me. I hate 'em. I've been trying to keep them out of the department but the minute I sell one Bloom whips off and orders another. Drives me crazy. They're hell for getting fingerprints; one grubby kid can cost me fifteen minutes polishing. The cannonball just needs the odd shot of Pledge. *(Notices ANNA staring at him.)* Is something wrong?

ANNA: What. Oh, sorry. *(Points to waterbed.)* Hoo—is that a waterbed?

WESLEY: Somewhat in the ritzy bracket.

ANNA: I'll say.

WESLEY: This baby and I have been together three years. I can't sell it to save my life and Bloom never lets me forget it. It's got a stereo, digital alarm... It undulates at the flick of a switch. *(Flips switch; nothing happens.)* It's supposed to undulate.

ANNA: *(Sitting on it.)* What do you call this?

WESLEY: No no, there's a little wave-maker inside. *(Kicks *bed, and will continue to do so, periodically.)* It's like a mini-water park. C'mon baby—

BLOOM: How's everything up there?

WESLEY: *(To ANNA.)* He's already bored silly—

BLOOM: Wesley! Can you hear me?

WESLEY: *(Going to intercom.)* I don't know how he's going to handle retirement. *(Into intercom.)* Everything's copacetic.

BLOOM: That's a revolting word. I wouldn't say "copacetic" to my worst enemy. I just wanted to convey a hot news flash: there are a couple of parties interested in the waterbed. They'll undoubtedly want to buy it, tomorrow. Do you catch my drift?

WESLEY: *(To ANNA, his hand over the mike.)* He's using psychology on you. *(Back to intercom.)* She seems to favour the cannonball.

BLOOM: And who can blame her. The cannonball's a lovely bed. But I'd feel "guilty" if I didn't warn her the waterbed's getting snapped up.

WESLEY: Roger, sir.

ANNA: *(As WESLEY hangs up intercom mike.)* Now tell me he's not cute. *(Going to the brass bed.)* So you're really against brass beds, eh.

WESLEY: It's just the fingerprints. Plus, if you like to sit up and read, the headframe freezes your back to death.

ANNA: They make me nostalgic. This one doesn't quite cut it, though. Don't you have anything more traditional?

WESLEY: Just what you see.

ANNA: So, tell me about the Dingles. How's married life treating them?

WESLEY: Not very well. They're divorced.

ANNA: Don't tell me—I can guess. Billy was having affairs of the heart.

WESLEY: You're about a foot north.

ANNA: I'm not surprised. Billy was born sleazy. All the time I was going with him he was sneaking around with your sister. *(Tragic.)* The milkshakes he was buying her. The peppermint Dentyne they were passing from mouth to mouth.

WESLEY: He was a creep deluxe. It was terrible for Jude.

ANNA: What's she doing now?

WESLEY: She's down in Toronto, working in computers.

ANNA: Who isn't.

WESLEY: Me.

ANNA: And me.

WESLEY: I mean, I.

ANNA: And I. See—some of Miss Eaton sunk in. *(Pause.)* You know, if you keep kicking that thing it'll spring a leak.

WESLEY: I want to make it undulate for you.

ANNA: It's OK. I'm not the waterbed type anyway.

WESLEY: What do you have now?

ANNA: A futon.

WESLEY: We never carried them. Mr. Bloom thinks they're a fad.

ANNA: *(Of the waterbed.)* And those aren't?

WESLEY: He owns the store.

ANNA: *(Sighing; lying on the brass bed.)* This is heaven. You know how you're not supposed to food shop on an empty stomach because when you hit the frozen cakes you'll blow the budget? Well, I'm bone tired. I want this one, now.

WESLEY: Really?

ANNA: On condition I don't have to move for twenty-four hours. I got back to town three days ago and I haven't stopped working. I'm staying at Mom's, but I've rented a place of my own and I spent all yesterday and today painting. It's a dump but it's in my son's school district, so he won't have to readjust. I mean, he's going to have to adjust to me, but this way his chums can stay the same.

WESLEY: What's his name?

ANNA: Jason.

WESLEY: Jason.

ANNA: And I know what you're thinking.

WESLEY: I'm not thinking anything!

ANNA: My Jason was the first. I pioneered the name. It's not my fault that four billion Jason Josh Joels followed mine. Anyway, the kid's been living with Mom while I've been at school. But she's seventy now and Jason's on the cusp of puberty. I cannot sentence my mother in her golden years to that.

WESLEY: You'd think it would get easier the older he gets.

ANNA: That boy's chock-full of hormones! His insides are like a microwave on full blast and he's about to blow the door off! *(Makes a booming noise.)*

WESLEY: Holy.

ANNA: Aw, he's a good kid, but I'm beat. I'm going to get the apartment in operation this weekend, then next

	week I'll set up an office and get some currency. So I can pay for this bed. Did I tell you I'm a lawyer?
WESLEY:	Your graduation notice was in the paper—congratulations!
ANNA:	Thanks. Mom placed it. It's good publicity, I guess. You wouldn't believe how proud she is.
WESLEY:	You're the first lawyer from our year.
ANNA:	"Our year"?
WESLEY:	Class of '71.
ANNA:	I didn't quite graduate.
WESLEY:	Neither did I, but it seemed like our year.
ANNA:	*(Sighs.)* I painted ten hours yesterday and another eight today. *(Relaxing on bed.)* Do you mind?
WESLEY:	Be my guest. There aren't any customers and Bloom can't get up the stairs anymore.
ANNA:	What's over there?
WESLEY:	The Lighting Department. I'm sort of in charge of it now too, but it's a disaster area. Bloom has this thing for swag lamps. The room's a jungle of dangling wires. You could get strangled, no probs.
ANNA:	How do you know I'm the only lawyer?
WESLEY:	I don't, for sure, but I know what most people are doing, from the paper, or sometimes they come in here. You hear. Birth announcements. They're all popping babies.
ANNA:	I went to the reunion, to network. You weren't there.
WESLEY:	That's because I didn't go. Technically we weren't eligible.

ANNA: Now you're the one being legalistic. Nobody challenged me. They stamped my hand and in I went, suffering a very bad case of déja vu.

WESLEY: I borrowed the neighbour's dog so I'd have an excuse to walk by the school. If Jude had come home I might've gone with her, but she figured Billy'd be there, so she stayed clear.

ANNA: He's fat.

WESLEY: Billy!?

ANNA: *(Gesturing.)* Humungus!

WESLEY: Excellent!

ANNA: They're all fat and bald. Not that it matters, of course.

WESLEY: The Examiner had a big write-up. I keep a scrapbook.

ANNA: You do.

WESLEY: Yeah. Stupid huh.

ANNA: You're kind of a bear for punishment.

WESLEY: It's interesting to see how people's lives unfold. Some I could've predicted. Others are surprises.

ANNA: Anyone famous yet?

WESLEY: I did a TV commercial once in a grass skirt. No, nobody's famous. There are two doctors though: Anne McAdam and Walter Robey—

ANNA: And Mary Lou Winters married one. How many d'you figure still live here?

WESLEY: No more than twenty-five.

ANNA: I'll send 'em business cards.

WESLEY: Jim Schull died in a car accident.

ANNA: You're kidding! Which was he?

WESLEY: Short guy, Coke bottle glasses?

ANNA: I can't picture him. Any family?

WESLEY: A wife, two kids.

ANNA: That's really sad. Did you know him?

WESLEY: Not really, but I still felt bad. *(As ANNA pulls a thread off his jacket.)* He never did anything against me. What're you doing?

ANNA: Sorry—it's the mother in me. You had a thread the size of a shoelace. Here's another one. *(Distracted; points to cannonball.)* Is this a queen?

WESLEY: Yes. We had it in one and a half, but it sold yesterday.

ANNA: What time is it?

WESLEY: A quarter to.

ANNA: You close at midnight?

WESLEY: Midnight madness. The clock's ticking and we're crazy for value.

ANNA: So I have fifteen minutes to choose. If I buy something tonight, will you deliver it tomorrow?

WESLEY: Pas doo problem.

ANNA: I'm climbing the walls at Mom's. She's in the Citi-Centre high-rise and I have to share a bedroom with Jason. Don't ever let anyone tell you thirteen year-olds can't snore. *(Surveys room.)* Decisions decisions. I'd be a real hit with Jace if I got the waterbed.

WESLEY: I thought it was your bed—

ANNA: Oh, it is, but Jason's at that age where it's important for his mom to look cool. His buddies have been coming 'round to inspect me. Mom's apartment was the gang's drop-in centre and the Grade Seven mafia's worried about the new regime.

WESLEY: *(Still kicking waterbed discreetly.)* Should they worry?

ANNA: In my less tired moments I think my house'll be a haven for them all. We'll sit around at night and make popcorn and I'll get my guitar out and teach them old Joni Mitchell songs. They'll be having so much fun they'll never haunt another plaza. That's when I'm rested. Right now I think that if just one of those fuzzy-lipped brats puts a sneaker over my threshold he'll never live to see Grade Eight.

WESLEY: *(A smile.)* Jason sounds like a lucky kid.

ANNA: Aw, we get along. *(Pause.)* That's too bad about Jude and Billy. I'm sorry they split.

WESLEY: I wasn't.

ANNA: There's something about them being divorced that offends my concept of rightness. They looked so good together. All that blondness. All those teeth. They were so cool.

WESLEY: But you were 'in'.

ANNA: Like Flynn, till I fell from grace. High school wasn't meant for you and me.

WESLEY: I know. We're the ones who blossom in later life. Every movie that's made on the subject has the high school heroes bombing out. Billy gets fat and you and I get to be president every time.

ANNA: That's lovely on celluloid—but explain Mary Lou Winters.

WESLEY: Yeah.

ANNA: Rich and popular then, even more so now. I sweat my way through law school—she marries the doctor and gets to lounge around Forest Heights for the rest of her life. Where's the justice?

WESLEY: She's miserable?

ANNA: Naw! She's happy as a clam! You should've seen her at the reunion. She was standing in the middle of the main hall and you could barely squeeze around her, the fur coat was that bulky. And a very handsome doctor was attached to the mink.

WESLEY: Did she recognize you?

ANNA: Immediately. "Which graduating class are you here with?" asked the dirty you-know-what. Well, we chatted for a few minutes—she never did introduce her doctor—and she made it very clear her behind was thoroughly in the butter. "And what about you, dear?" she asked finally, as if she cared. Guess what I did. I'd had cards printed up and I handed her one. "Mary Lou," I said. "I'm a lawyer. I do divorce work. Call me when sawbones here dumps you."

WESLEY: Excellent!

ANNA: God did it feel good. I turned around and whipped off and the triumph lasted oh ten feet, until I remembered Mary Lou was going home to a mansion in Forest Heights and crawling into bed with a gorgeous doctor, whereas I... (Shakes head.)

WESLEY: But you scored the telling blow!

ANNA: Not really. Mary Lou yelled after me, "I heard that line on TV!"

WESLEY: Yelled?

ANNA: Like a goddamn foghorn. Once a cheerleader, always a cheerleader. You could've heard her in the science wing. *(Pause; of the brass bed:)* I think I'll go with the brass.

WESLEY: I'd take the cannonball if I were—

ANNA: I like brass. OK, OK I'll sleep on it. *(Elbows WESLEY.)* That's a Bed Department joke. Hey— what kind of salesman are you, anyway, telling me not to buy something! How've you lasted a decade in sales?

WESLEY: Longer than that even. I've been here ten years and before that I was at Sears. Four years. Garden Supplies, so I'm up on my hoses, too.

ANNA: Are you on commission?

WESLEY: Partly. It's not much of a living. I mean, you hear what a real estate agent makes in a good year—you have to wonder.

ANNA: It's unusual to work so long in one place.

WESLEY: It never occurred to me to leave. That's not true—I decided once I'd go back to school so I could get into computers like Jude but cripes—I can barely plug in a toaster. When a three-prong plug is high tech…

ANNA: What part of town do you live in?

WESLEY: East city, just below the hill. Same place as always.

ANNA: You still live at home?

WESLEY: Sort of. It's mine now. Mom died a year ago.

ANNA: I'm sorry.

WESLEY: And Dad died when I was eight.

ANNA: You have a whole house…

WESLEY: Yeah, I'm an orphan.

ANNA: I'd kill for a whole house. You wanna marry me?

WESLEY: It's actually not a big house.

             They laugh.

ANNA: Aw darn, rejected again. Do you see Jude often?

WESLEY: Not really. We still phone on Sundays and she comes down for Christmas and Easter, but that's about it. I'll tell her you're back in town. She's still curious about what everyone's doing. You should've heard her when she found out Mary Lou Winters was living up in Forest Heights. "That bitch climbed that hill on her back!" Sorry.

ANNA: Jude always had a way with words.

WESLEY: Anyway, that's about it for me. It's kind of embarrassing there's so little to tell.

ANNA: Better too little than too much.

WESLEY: I don't know. Sometimes I feel like I've spent fifteen years sort of treading water. You know, Jesus fed crowds but Wesley sold beds.

BLOOM: Attention shoppers. Bloom's Furniture is going to close for the evening. All shoppers should hurry up and buy what she wants.

WESLEY: I told you I was an orphan? (*Intercom.*) Yes sir. Everything's fine.

BLOOM: And that discerning young lady is still admiring our beds?

WESLEY: Yes sir.

BLOOM: There may be some salient factors about those beds you've forgotten to mention.

WESLEY: Such as?

BLOOM: Perhaps you could come downstairs for a moment please?

WESLEY: But Mr. Bloom—

BLOOM: "To obey is better than sacrifice; and to hearken than the fat of rams." Get the hell down here.

WESLEY: I'll just be a sec. Maybe you'd like to pick out a lamp. I could throw in a swag with the cannonball. *(Intercom.)* I'm on my way.

          WESLEY starts to leave, then remembers he's left the intercom speaker on. He returns, and switches it off. ANNA pokes about; she can kick the waterbed, primp for a second in front of a mirror, and look into the swag room. Finally she can't resist—she switches the intercom speaker back on.

BLOOM: Tell her you'll give her that waterbed for 50 percent.

WESLEY: She doesn't want it.

BLOOM: Throw in some art. We have to get rid of the damn thing.

WESLEY: Take it home for Mrs. Bloom.

BLOOM: She gets motion sick from taking a bath. What'm I going to do with a waterbed left over?

WESLEY: It won't undulate. Anyway, she's nibbling at the cannonball.

BLOOM: That, I can unload at my brother's store. The waterbed calls for a sucker.

WESLEY: She's way too smart.

BLOOM: At fifty percent even a professor can't resist.

WESLEY: But sir.

BLOOM: Try. For me. For Bloom's. Once more into the

	breach. Once more 'round the mulberry bush. See. I can talk like you. A waterbed for posterity.
ANNA:	*(Picking up mike.)* Beds to Bloom. Beds to Bloom. I don't care how cute you are, I'm not shelling out for plastic-wrapped water.
BLOOM:	Don't be hasty.
ANNA:	This is taste, not haste.
WESLEY:	Anna—think. What Jesus walked on, you can sleep on.
BLOOM:	Wesley! *(To ANNA.)* Young lady, fifty percent off.
ANNA:	You add a dozen disciples, I'll consider it a deal. Which reminds me—will you send the stallion back up?
BLOOM:	Stallion?
ANNA:	The guy in the sweater.
BLOOM:	*(Long pause.)* Wesley?
ANNA:	That's the man. While I've got you on the line, Mr. Bloom—you want to explain that room full of swag lamps?
BLOOM:	What about them?
ANNA:	Who buys 'em?
BLOOM:	Citizens.
ANNA:	Of what planet?
BLOOM:	Ashburnham. There's a vast market for swag lamps.
ANNA:	Wesley worries about strangulation.
BLOOM:	Wesley worries for recreation.

WESLEY has entered and he reaches for the intercom mike. ANNA hands it back, after a moment's tease.

WESLEY: You've got the nerve of a canal horse.

ANNA: Sorry—I couldn't resist.

WESLEY: This is a store, you know. We've got an image of professionalism to maintain. *(Beginning to laugh.)* It's not funny. OK. It's mildly amusing.

BLOOM: What's going on up there?

WESLEY: Stallion?! What's he gonna think? You're really terrible. *(Over the intercom.)* Sir: the customer has been apprehended. I've got her tied to the cannonball.

BLOOM: Wesley. You shouldn't even joke.

ANNA: I just love the way he talks.

BLOOM: I'm locking up now. You could shoot a cannon down George Street.

WESLEY: Want some help with the cash?

BLOOM: What cash? Will you see the young lady out, whenever?

WESLEY: Yes sir.

BLOOM: Bless you, son.

WESLEY: *(Putting down the mike.)* He sounded tired, didn't he.

ANNA: It must be really draining on him. This place is an institution.

WESLEY: It had to happen. Bloom's survived for fifty years, but now—

ANNA: There's nobody to carry on?

WESLEY: One son, Jay, is a doctor in Texas, and Ronny's a
              lawyer. We thought Ronny would take over—he
              used to work here summers—but Bloom didn't
              want him in retail, and apparently he's doing well
              in Toronto. Bloom's lonely. His wife isn't much
              company, she's busy with this and that, and he's
              got boo-all except the store.

ANNA: It's sad.

WESLEY: It's different for me because I'll get another job.
              He's going to retire and rot. I don't know how he'll
              stand coming downtown even, because he'll see
              this place sitting here, a big empty hulk... Anyway,
              we're having a farewell bash. Nothing major. Just
              me, the Blooms, the part-timers, assorted spouses.
              Ronny's coming back and, for a surprise, I've
              invited all the retired employees I could trace.
              We're going to have some of Bloom's home-made
              hooch, crank up the muzak and have a big pajama
              party. If there are any beds left.

ANNA: Isn't anybody buying the building?

WESLEY: It's a white elephant. Maybe they'll make it a bingo
              hall. The only things that survive down here
              anymore are the specialty boutiques. Eaton's
              vamoosed to the mall, so did Woolworth's.

ANNA: And the supermarket's gone! I went there today
              and—

WESLEY: They couldn't get extra parking. Someday you'll
              drive down George Street and there'll be this giant
              cobweb strung across the road. I'm under no
              illusions. I've gone out to the malls and strolled
              around the furniture stores. They feel cleaner.
              They're all on one floor.

ANNA: And you have to admit, some of this stuff is pretty
              godawful!

WESLEY: It's not that bad!

ANNA: The Hall of Swag?

WESLEY: Yeah. But those malls—they ain't Bloom's. There's only one Bloom's in the whole world. There's something to be said for those stairs you climbed –

ANNA: Dangerous?

WESLEY: And worn into curves by fifty years of shoppers. Look at that ceiling.

ANNA: Pressed tin!

WESLEY: When did you last see that? In the office there's a whole wall of family portraits—Bloom's parents and his family, a photo of the town in Russia they came from. Ah, I don't know, we've been done in by the chains. I know it's evolution, the fittest survive and all that but there's still nothing wrong with mourning a store like this—nobody's going to cry when a chain dies. They just get bigger and more anonymous, the cash they rake in flows out of town and out of the country, and when the money dries up they leave and nobody gives a damn. It all started with Kentucky Fried Chicken.

ANNA: (Pause.) Do you think it's kind of for the better?

WESLEY: What do you mean.

ANNA: For you.

WESLEY: (Wary.) Why.

ANNA: Because—

WESLEY: Since when is losing your job "kind of for the better"?

ANNA: It'll you know; push you out, into the real world.

WESLEY: Why the hell does everyone think this place isn't

real? You and Jude—you're a pair. This place may
be dying but it's real enough. It's a lot more real
than some plastic damn mall. If that's what you
think is real, then I don't know what the hell you're
doing here.

ANNA: Getting a bargain from a grouchy salesman?

WESLEY: Get your bargains at Nutty Normans! Go buy your
bed there! Then you can rest assured you could get
the same deal coast to coast, that oughta make it a
touch more real for you. I mean, if something's real
once, if you repeat it a thousand times it must be
even more so, eh!?

ANNA: Wait a second.

WESLEY: I'm sick of people telling me—

ANNA: WES! Wes! I want a bed; I just want to buy a bed.
All right?

WESLEY: Sorry.

ANNA: It's OK.

WESLEY: I don't normally chew out customers. I'm really
tired, I guess.

ANNA: That makes two of us. I'll buy a bed and take off.
(Points to cannonball.) That one gets the nod.

WESLEY: You wanted the brass.

ANNA: I've changed my mind. But we're going to haggle.
If Bloom was giving me fifty percent off the
waterbed, I don't see why I can't have the same on
the cannonball.

WESLEY: We can still move this. It may go tomorrow.

ANNA: Give me a minute. *(Pause.)* You know, you really
have to wonder at Council letting all those malls
get built, don't you.

WESLEY: Council's preoccupied with growth. It's all they talk about. It was less than one percent last year. Now they want five. But who needs growth? If you want my opinion, the nation with a plummeting growth rate is making an important environmental contribution to the world. *(Starting to orate.)* If the human race is serious about surviving, I say we should be trying to decrease our economies, so we're using up less resources.

ANNA: Fewer.

WESLEY: Thank you Miss Eaton. Anyway, you know what I mean. Less is best. That's why Trudeau was such a great statesman—he wrecked the economy.

ANNA: I doubt Mulroney's going to do much better.

WESLEY: Then he'll be a great statesman too. Anna—do you ever think you think too much?

ANNA: I'm usually too busy, and I'm not really of that bent. Deep down, I'm pretty shallow. I used to kid myself in high school I was a thinker. I'd sit in the bleachers and ponder the nature of cheerleading.

WESLEY: No.

ANNA: Yes. I'd look at your sister bouncing up and down so earnestly and I'd try to figure out why an intelligent girl like Jude would go in for all that tribal craziness.

WESLEY: Any conclusions?

ANNA: Tons. All those male hormones were being sweated out in violent endeavour on the field—there has to be a reason. Guys don't make mincemeat of each other for the good of their health, and one lousy trophy at the end of the season isn't much of an incentive, either. No, there had to be another reason, and Jude and her squad of cheerleaders supplied it. I'd watch them wiggle and do the splits—and I understood. Football is symbolic foreplay.

WESLEY: Makes sense.

ANNA: And the pompoms. Have you ever noticed how the cheerleaders grab 'em and shake 'em and hang on to the things for dear life? And all the while they look very, very happy? It's the high point of their lives because they've finally got total control over something very, very important!

WESLEY: Oh no—

ANNA: Yes! Pompoms are symbolic testicles!

WESLEY: Oh my God.

ANNA: Told you I was shallow. One Grade Eleven textbook on tribal sociology and you just heard the sordid results. Naw, thinking stinks. I'm right off it. It's brought me nothing but heartache. I spent all of law school living with a two hundred pound lump of theory.

WESLEY: You've lost me.

ANNA: Albert. Albert Potter. He was a great guy but he theoried me to death. Albert couldn't stop thinking. He couldn't butter toast without pondering the significance of a knife wiping yellow stuff over a crispy surface.

WESLEY: You're making this up.

ANNA: Was the knife symbolic of society, rubbing a patina of civilization over something fundamentally inhospitable? And, if butter was civilization— what was jam?

WESLEY: Now I know you're making it up.

ANNA: I only wish.

WESLEY:	Did Jason live with you and Albert?
ANNA:	I couldn't afford it. I had to work part-time to put myself through school, so Jace stayed here with Mom. She'd bus him down every weekend, or I'd come up. Actually, Jason was the clincher. Albert couldn't even feed Jason without trying to lure him into some discussion like, "Why did dinosaurs go extinct?" Or, "If you left a robot outside during a rainstorm, would the robot cry?"
WESLEY:	Cry? That's interesting. I wonder how you could tell. I mean, the rain—
ANNA:	Don't you start! Aw, a kid can't have a theoretical dad. I had to break it off. Three years down the tubes. Albert was really upset—and here's the shocker—"I'm not crying over you, Anna," he announces. "Don't flatter yourself. It's Jason I'm gonna miss." And Jason took it hard, too. I mean, I thought they lived on different planets but somehow they'd developed this bond. How on earth did I get on this?!
WESLEY:	You came in to buy a bed.
ANNA:	And somehow we got on to theory. My specialty. It's good to talk to an adult.
WESLEY:	Yeah.
ANNA:	It's like everyone in Ashburnham's lined up for the ark. They're all in twos and there aren't enough of us square pegs to form a queue in any other direction. But—"It's a great place to raise kids!"
BLOOM:	*(Intercom.)* Bloom to Beds. Bloom to Beds.
ANNA:	I thought he went home—
WESLEY:	*(Going to mike.)* Yes sir?
BLOOM:	I've finished the cash. It's under the you-know-what. Is that young lady still there?

WESLEY: She's still making up her mind.

BLOOM: She's not holding you hostage?

WESLEY: No sir.

BLOOM: I'd hate for us to get robbed our second last day.

WESLEY: I think we're safe.

BLOOM: I'm going then. Don't leave the stockroom light on this time.

WESLEY: No sir.

BLOOM: You forgot last night. It's a waste.

WESLEY: All shall be doused on the western front.

BLOOM: My son, will you ever talk normal? Still, I'm going to miss it. But I'm an old man, so now it's home I go. Good night. And good night customer.

ANNA: *(Waves at intercom.)* 'Night.

WESLEY: Shalom sir.

BLOOM: *(Long sigh.)* O God our help in ages past.

WESLEY: Mazel Tov.

BLOOM: A-men brother.

WESLEY: Mr. Bloom?

BLOOM: I know.

BLOOM &
WESLEY: Next year in Jerusalem.

                        WESLEY hangs up mike.

ANNA: That was interesting.

WESLEY: It's our good night routine. I act Jewish, he acts Protestant. It's for luck.

ANNA: Of course.

WESLEY: One night I wished him Mazel Tov and the next day we sold a colonial four-poster that'd been sitting here for two years.

ANNA: So why does he talk Protestant?

WESLEY: It moves the velvet paintings.

ANNA: I don't know Wes—

WESLEY: Not that anyone's religious. Actually, Bloom was, but they closed the synagogue on him. You have to have ten men, sort of like a quorum, but they were down to seven. And I used to go too—to church that is—I'm Presbyterian, but I quit. It was hard for me to give up the concept of life after death. It meant I had to start going to the gym.

ANNA: I've followed everything up till that.

WESLEY: It was my theory that I'd come back in the next life, well, as a big stud. Like Billy, only with the ability to eat without scratching. It's a common theory of afterlife. You get reincarnated upwards: rooster to cow, cow to Wesley, Wesley to—big stud. So when I gave up religion, I had to face the bitter truth: I wasn't ever going to reincarnate. I would never be a sex god in my next life. And, if I only had one life to live that meant I only had one body to live it in— I joined the Y the next day.

ANNA: It shows.

WESLEY: Huh?

ANNA: You look a lot better than you did in high school.

WESLEY: Bull.

ANNA: I'm not kidding. Your shoulders are really quite broad and—

WESLEY: Stop it OK.

ANNA: I just said I thought you were looking—

WESLEY: I heard you.

ANNA: It was a compliment!

WESLEY: Look. Do you want a bed? I'll sell you a bed.

ANNA: Excuse me for living.

WESLEY: *(Pause.)* Sorry. I thought you were making fun of
               me.

ANNA: By saying you look good?

WESLEY: *(Pause.)* Why'd you come here?

ANNA: I smell a trick question. Because I want to buy a
               bed?

WESLEY: No, why'd you come back to Ashburnham. You
               didn't have to, so why did you?

ANNA: That's not very loyal to the town that bred and
               raised you.

WESLEY: I just mean you could've stayed in Toronto; there's
               lots of people there. Unmarried ones. Jude's
               always got a party on or something. You could've
               moved Jason down there.

ANNA: I didn't have a social life in Toronto, so I'm not
               losing anything by moving here. Mom's here and I
               think it's healthier in Ashburnham. If the kid and I
               had to make a go of it in Toronto we'd be locked
               away in some high-rise out in the suburbs and
               Jason'd be into God knows what. Which he's into
               here, no doubt, but on a more modest scale.

WESLEY: I still don't understand why you came back.

ANNA: Aw, I don't like sounding like the holy martyr all
               the time, but I'm here because Jason's here. I'm not

uprooting him any more than I have to. He'll be finished high school in six years—if he wants to move then, we will. But he's got to have roots somewhere and his, well, they're here.

WESLEY: But if the roots aren't good—

ANNA: Bad roots?

WESLEY: Not "bad". I mean, not good. Not good as in not-good-different, I think.

ANNA: You better explain.

WESLEY: I guess I mean I wonder if letting Jason have roots like you say is going to make up for him being denied a father.

ANNA: That's a neat little judgmental turd. I "denied" him a father?

WESLEY: No no, I meant life denied him. Events. Same way I got gypped.

ANNA: And now it's "gypped".

WESLEY: I meant sort of –

ANNA: I think you meant gypped. That's what you said.

WESLEY: That guy in law school—Albert—he would've married you.

ANNA: I'm supposed to get married so Jason can have a father.

WESLEY: You said Albert loved Jason. They had a bond. Maybe we shouldn't talk about this—

ANNA: I want to tell you something. People get married because they love each other, not because they happen to love the same third person.

WESLEY: You might have come to love Albert, in time.

ANNA: Not as a life partner. No.

WESLEY: But you're not sure.

ANNA: Of course I'm not sure. That's something you're never sure of.

WESLEY: Some people seem to know.

ANNA: What the living hell would you know? You're a goddamn Presbyterian nun! Look. I have been through hell and back for that son of mine. I've been through hell to become a lawyer, school, school, more school, articling, Bar Ads, part-time jobs and every extra minute, every free minute I had I came home and spent it with Jason. No matter how much I wanted to go out with my girlfriends, or on a date...no matter how—

WESLEY: You didn't have to become a lawyer.

ANNA: You're right. I could've sold beds.

WESLEY: There's nothing wrong with selling beds.

ANNA: There's something wrong with hiding under them. I'm having a real problem here. You can't stir your ass out of this place to save your life but me, I'm supposed to forget any aspirations I might have— I'm supposed to marry some guy I don't love— what's the use. You're not the first one to say I've gypped him. Aren't you going to tell me I should've put him up for adoption? I get that thrown at me, too. Well, you don't have the right. You just don't have the right. Not you, not this town, not anyone. Look at you. Where the hell do you get off judging me. I'd've thought that you, of all people, you, Weirdley, you'd be above that. You're pathetic. No sale. No sale. I'm history.

               ANNA storms out. WESLEY stands frozen; shocked.

WESLEY: Anna. Anna. *(Louder.)* Anna! Wait! *(Runs after her, to the doorway.)* Anna! Don't go! *(Runs to mike, speaks into it.)* Anna! Anna! *(Slams mike down.)* Jesus. Jesus Christ, she's gone. *(Runs to window; tries unsuccessfully to pull it open.)* Get back here dammit! You can't walk out—open, come on, open—*(Looks down street.)* Where is she?! Anna! Anna!

> *WESLEY is now angry, and directs that anger at objects as he returns to the room. He might rip diplomas off walls, pound pillows and he delivers an especially vicious kick to the waterbed.*

Aw to hell with it, you're just like everybody else, so go to hell. Go to hell Anna Bregner, I hate you. I hate you all. I hate this place. *(Pause.)* I'm through. I'm through. No more Bloom's, no more Bed Department, no more beds, no more goddamn swags, no more cannonball, no more brass... *(Reaches the desk, pulls out a letter opener and begins stalking the waterbed.)* So. So. No one wants you, eh. You've been up here a little too long, eh. Well, it's time you earned your goddamned keep. Time we put you to good use. Maybe we'll just forget our little Midnight Madness Sale. Maybe we'll have ourselves a Water Damage Sale! Time to die my undulating little friend. *(Begins to raise letter opener.)* Speak, hands for me!

> *WESLEY is poised to stab the bed. ANNA rounds the corner.*

ANNA: Wesley, stop!

WESLEY: Anna!

WESLEY falls to bed in surprise.

As he does: fast black.

End of Act One.

Act Two

Lights up. WESLEY has fallen on the waterbed and managed to avoid stabbing it.

ANNA: Are you OK?

WESLEY: You came back!

ANNA: Wes—are you—

WESLEY: Yes. No. I don't know. You came back. I thought you went.

ANNA: I never actually got outside—are you sure you're OK? You sounded—I mean, you were going to kill that thing.

WESLEY: Sorry.

ANNA: It's not a crime to get mad.

WESLEY: Sorry. *(Beat.)* Why am I apologizing? You stormed out of here and never let me finish what I was trying to say. We were having a good time and then whammo, out you go, and I'm alone *(Clicks fingers.)* just like that, I'm alone. You have any idea what that's like?

ANNA: Yes.

WESLEY: No. No you don't, you don't have a clue, it's easy for you to run out of here, you've got someplace to run to. You've got people: your Mom, Jason—

ANNA: But you've got Jude, your—

WESLEY: And my what. What have I got? I'll tell you what
           I've got. Nothing. Nada. No one. When there's a
           symphony night I buy two tickets. I show up at the
           high school, they hand me my tickets and I shrug
           and say, "My friend's sick. I only need one." So
           they won't know. I've only got one pillow on my
           bed—why would I ever expect a guest head? Some
           nights I lie there and look at the map I've got up on
           the wall beside my bed and I count all the dots that
           are cities and I wonder, "How many Wesleys are
           there in this goddamn country? How many others
           are lying there, alone, wondering what'd be like to
           have a real human being breathing beside them?"
           In the winter, I don't shovel the walk. Why would
           I? The only ones using it are me, the neighbours'
           kids flogging chocolate bars, Jehovah's Witnesses.
           Winter progresses, there's just this one deepening
           groove, one person wide, one neat path to my door
           that I follow up and down, up and down, up and
           down, until thaw… One skinny little path, up and
           down—

ANNA: I understand.

WESLEY: How could you?

ANNA: There's more than one kind of lonely. You've got
           one kind, I've got another. I've got a family but I
           don't have anyone—to talk to—you know—like an
           adult, a friend… So what do I do with the first one
           I meet? I blow my stack. I got downstairs—oh I just
           feel sick about what I said, Wes, I'm truly sorry.

WESLEY: For what?

ANNA: Come on, for being a witch, for saying—

WESLEY: Everything you said was true. I am pathetic. That
           was a good word. You must take me for the biggest
           idiot in the world.

ANNA: That's not what I think at all.

WESLEY: I can never say what I'm thinking. Not when it's important. I want to say something and it just doesn't come out. I wanted to tell you I admire you. For coming back here, for facing everyone, for not letting things get you down, or screw you up, for being brave—

ANNA: That's a laugh.

WESLEY: You've raised a son on your own and done it well. That's brave. I could never have done that.

ANNA: Who says I've done it well? I've been an absentee parent. Sure—Jason's a good kid—right now—but what's to stop him becoming a mess later? I don't know if I've—if I've been around him enough to instill any values—

WESLEY: Sure you have.

ANNA: Enough to keep him out of trouble? Don't admire me for being a successful parent. The jury's still out on that one. And I'm not brave. I'm terrified. I don't know if the kid and I can get it together, and he's all I've got. Jason is it. No, I'm not brave... We have a lot in common, you and I. We're both lonely, we're both scared. Maybe it is harder for you. You live alone, you work here alone. And this place, this room, it's kind of a time warp. I don't mean that negatively, just that—

WESLEY: It's only one more day.

ANNA: But all those years.

WESLEY: I chose it. At least, I think I chose it. You make your bed...

ANNA: The last time I was up here, it was with Dan. Nothing's changed in fourteen years. Well—you're here. Dan was Jason's father. We weren't actually looking for a bed—that would've been

	politically incorrect. Just a mattress. Who was selling up here then?
WESLEY:	Probably Mr. Bishop. Tall, gaunt?
ANNA:	Ichabod Cranish?
WESLEY:	*(A laugh.)* That's him.
ANNA:	He looked at us pretty dimly. I was seventeen. Maybe he was just being sniffy because we only wanted a mattress, but Dan thought he was laying a morality trip on us.
WESLEY:	He was jealous.
ANNA:	You think so?
WESLEY:	Everyone who comes up here is happy. People buy beds for happy reasons—they're setting up house or they've just moved in with someone or they've worn out their old bed. People like coming to bed departments. Do you—do you like sherry?
ANNA:	Hate it.
WESLEY:	Oh.
ANNA:	Why?
WESLEY:	I uh I sometimes have a glass after closing.
ANNA:	How posh. Go ahead—don't let me stop you.
WESLEY:	*(Producing two styrofoam cups.)* You know, you haven't lived until you've tasted sherry out of styrofoam.
ANNA:	Twist my arm. I don't suppose you've got some pretzels. I missed dinner.
WESLEY:	Chocolate-topped digestives.
ANNA:	With sherry?

WESLEY: It's an acquired taste.

ANNA: Let's give her a shot.

WESLEY: I used to have a Coke after closing with Mr. Hamilton, when he ran Lighting. After he retired, I upped the ante.

ANNA: This isn't bad.

WESLEY: It's good stuff. I don't have a lot of indulgences, but this, and the digestives, are two.

ANNA: Wes. *(Holds up cup.)* Up your ante. *(They clink.)* You know, it was all your sister's fault I even met Dan.

WESLEY: Why?

ANNA: Jude and I made a pact to get stoned on her seventeenth birthday, so we went down to War Memorial Park to buy dope. Jude didn't want to buy it at school because she was a cheerleader and—nice girls don't smoke pot.

WESLEY: Sounds like a book title.

ANNA: We went down to the park one night but your big bold sister chickened out so I went in alone.

WESLEY: Weren't you scared?

ANNA: Petrified. I asked the first hippie I met for a "nickel bag". I knew that much—it's five bucks worth. And then—I kind of stayed there, in the park. It was barely spring but it was full of people— somebody was sitting on the steps of the statue, tapping a tambourine. There were little circles of people sitting around, talking, smoking up—in downtown Ashburnham! And that's when I met Dan. He was wearing an Indian shirt, beads, the whole number, bare feet... He had these gentle, wicked eyes—woof, I was a goner.

Self-conscious now.

See—as I said—it's good to talk to an adult. Just make sure this stays out of the scrapbook.

WESLEY: It'll cost you a bed.

ANNA: *(Indicating waterbed.)* Not the—

            WESLEY nods.

You're a cruel man, Wesley Marshall. *(Pause.)* So anyway, I hung out at the park a lot over the next few months. Somehow I became "Dan's woman"—this was pre-feminism, remember. It was pretty weird for a high school girl. I was going steady and I didn't even know it. I suppose I could've guessed—Dan always passed me the joint first.

WESLEY: Your mother must've been going nuts.

ANNA: She was working crazy hours at the hospital—she never knew.

WESLEY: I don't understand why you'd pick a hippie. Why not a football hero?

ANNA: Dan was a lot more exciting than anyone at Ashburnham High. And it wasn't only him—there was a whole group of new people, new music, poetry. Dan wrote poetry! Can you imagine Billy writing a poem? Dan was a sociology major— theories galore. You know me and theoretical men. He had ideas about society and education and an endless supply of ideas about sex. That's another thing about Dan—he was the first guy who didn't treat me like I was inventory. Billy—he was next thing to a rapist, an octopus. With Dan I was getting respect and no pressure. You know, I look at Jace and I pray to God he never turns into one of those high school hornballs. I've got to teach him girls aren't for pawing.

WESLEY: Good luck.

ANNA: You didn't paw.

WESLEY: I didn't date. I wanted to, I just didn't know how to set the whole process in motion.

ANNA: You want the truth? Jude asked me if she could ask you to ask me to the Grade Twelve prom.

WESLEY: That would've been some disaster. I didn't even know how to dance. You'd have been embarrassed.

ANNA: Hell, I'd have got us stoned out of our gourds. That would've given them something to talk about. You in a tux, me in chiffon, floating down the receiving line. Good evening, Principal Wilson. And hey, groovy dress Miss Eaton.

WESLEY: *(Having fun.)* Like hey man, Anna, it's like Camelot man.

                    Shared laugh.

ANNA: You're right. It wouldn't have worked. So—you have any other indulgences?

WESLEY: Not really. I read like a maniac.

ANNA: Me too, when I have time. I'm fighting my way through Faulkner.

WESLEY: I love Faulkner! Which one are you reading?

ANNA: "Absalom, Absalom"!

                    Mutual groan.

WESLEY: *(Southern accent.)* It's tough sleddin', ain't it?

ANNA: But I try, suh, I try. Dan was a big reader too. He used to sit in the park and read his brains out. Well, first he'd smoke 'em out, then he'd read 'em out. He told me he could read *Ulysses* stoned.

WESLEY: You can't even read it unstoned! Jeez—if I'd
                 known you could read in that park—

ANNA: You could do anything there.

WESLEY: I don't recall seeing anyone reading. I had to walk
                 through there on the way home from the library
                 and I'm sorry—I don't remember seeing any
                 books. Do you know how hard it was walking by
                 those people—when you know you're being
                 watched and you're trying to walk normal but
                 your knees lock, your bum petrifies—

ANNA: Can you imagine if you'd ever stopped and had a
                 toke?

WESLEY: The gap between the sidewalk and the park
                 benches wasn't for me to cross.

ANNA: It was a very accepting time.

WESLEY: In retrospect.

ANNA: I was there. It was different. And that's not just
                 rose-coloured glasses.

WESLEY: Then why didn't it last?

ANNA: It was too gentle. We had to turn our backs on it for
                 self-preservation. But it's still in me. I'm waiting.
                 One of these days, Jupiter and Mars are going to
                 realign—and Anna Bregner will be ready.

WESLEY: But you're a lawyer!

ANNA: I'll cover my briefcase in flower decals.

                     Holds out cup.

WESLEY: More?

ANNA: Why not.

WESLEY: *(Pouring.)* Where's Dan now?

ANNA:	Out west, running a group home. He'd be great at it. When I met him he was manager of the Y Drop-in Centre.
WESLEY:	I never went.
ANNA:	No one from our school did.
WESLEY:	Didn't you have to be on a bad trip?
ANNA:	That was the Crisis Centre. We were just drop-in. We played music, had non-competitive sports, did crafts. Talk about another era! I can't imagine Jason and his buddies getting into beadwork! Do you remember Magic Meadows? We were the organizers. The name was my idea.
WESLEY:	Mom fought that that thing like crazy.
ANNA:	All the neighbours did.
WESLEY:	She was convinced there'd be a mass orgy up there and we'd have drug-crazed hippies spilling into our backyard, doing rude things to her rose-bushes.
ANNA:	(Laughs.) All that opposition made it hell to organize. We had to build outhouses because nobody'd rent them to us. We had a hassle-free first aid tent and a volunteer clean-up crew. There was a vegetarian kitchen—
WESLEY:	—And the music. Whew!
ANNA:	Yeah.
WESLEY:	We could hear it down the hill. All over the city, for that matter.
ANNA:	We booked the biggies: Major Hooples, Little Caesar, Mandala—
WESLEY:	I snuck up the hill and watched from the trees.

ANNA: You should've joined us!

WESLEY: After the crusading Mom did, I'd have felt like
               Benedict Arnold. I'm sure she had the festival
               under surveillance. She probably had her bridge
               club in disguise, slipping through the crowds,
               taking photos with their Brownies.

ANNA: It was an incredible day. It really worked. It was so
               peaceful, so unlike anything we'd ever had here.

WESLEY: Mom was really disappointed nothing evil
               happened.

ANNA: We ended it exactly at nightfall, as ordered by
               Council. The clean-up brigade was too stoned, so
               Dan and I ended up raking the lawns and bagging
               everything. I didn't care. I was so happy—I
               belonged. We went back to Dan's. He lived in one
               of those big student houses near the cathedral, on
               Fleming Place. He had the whole top floor, it was
               the attic really, but he'd fixed it up. There was a
               balcony with doors that opened. Our mattress was
               right there, so we were half outside. If it rained it'd
               get damp—

WESLEY: Oh jeez, I can't condone bed abuse.

ANNA: A half hour ago you were all set to murder one.
               You'll be relieved to know we eventually got wise
               and put up a little awning. And there was a
               Manitoba maple growing up the front of the
               house—its leaves were like a curtain and that was
               wonderful in the mornings because the sun would
               come through. Or, if there was a moon, there'd be a
               back glow…

WESLEY: It sounds nice.

ANNA: Yeah. It rained finally that night. We woke about
               four or five, to the drumming on the roof. And
               there were pigeons in the eaves; they made pigeon

noises which actually kind of sound like you know, people making love, which might have given us the idea. *(Embarrassed now, a bit.)* Anyway, we did—make love—and Jason got the nod. That was the night, I'm sure that was the night. *(Pause.)* Do you understand about my boy now?

WESLEY: I think so.

ANNA: That summer with Dan was the first time in my life—it was the only time—when I just threw up my hands and said, "Let the chips fall where they may, I'm going with the flow." Remember that expression? Jason was conceived on the very best night of my best summer, with a man I loved—so I have to ask you, Wes, how many kids get a head-start like that?

WESLEY: I'm glad you've told me all this. I—we all tend to be—I can be judgmental. You heard me earlier. My sister would've had you in New York in ten minutes flat.

ANNA: Having an abortion? Mom and I discussed it but, I don't know, I guess it's one of those things I can accept for other people but not for me. And you know, there's hardly a day goes by that I don't thank God I kept him. Even when I'm dead tired and he's pissing me off. Which is often. Anyway, the rest is history. I started Grade Thirteen but, by October, I knew the jig was up and school seemed a bit irrelevant. I was still with Dan. You can't imagine how weird it is being pregnant in high school. I'd be in the girls' can and hear them talking about sex—some were speculating; others were having sex but not fun and, well, I was having both. I didn't have to worry about getting pregnant anymore, did I. With that load off my shoulders— well! School activities seemed really dumb. Everything seemed dumb. *(Pause.)* Inevitably the names started. Do you remember what they called me?

WESLEY: Yes.

ANNA: I don't know how they found out so fast. I wasn't
             showing.

WESLEY: You only had to tell one person.

ANNA: Mary Lou Winters.

WESLEY: Who told my sister. Who told Billy. The minute
             news like that crosses to the other sex –

ANNA: Pincushion. Pincushion Bregner. If it didn't
             represent so much loathing, it'd almost be funny.

WESLEY: It could never be funny.

ANNA: At the start I was never too sure what I was
             hearing—there'd be a cough at the back of the class
             (Coughs.) Pincushion—then giggles. Snickers. I'd
             catch people's eyes flickering down to my
             stomach, real fast, then up again. Mary Lou and
             your sister and everyone else stopped walking
             with me between classes. What, did they think they
             could catch it? Aw, I should've just quit but Mom
             wanted me to go as long as possible. Then, one
             morning in December, about three weeks before
             Christmas, I opened my locker and there were
             condoms draped over my books. A half dozen.
             They looked used, it was probably just spit, it
             doesn't matter. It was the hatred behind it.

WESLEY: I knew all this.

ANNA: I stood in front of my locker. I just stood there,
             staring. I didn't know what to do. I felt ashamed,
             grossed out—then angry. Really angry. I couldn't
             touch them and I wasn't going to remove them, not
             with everyone hanging about—and I didn't know
             how many were in on it but not a damn one of them
             was going to have the satisfaction of watching me
             clean my locker. So I marched down to see Vice
             Principal Whatshisname—

WESLEY: Tomlinson—

ANNA: He already knew I was pregnant. How the hell he found out, I'll never know. I said, "Sir, there are some things in my locker I want removed and I'm not doing it." I told him point blank what they were.

WESLEY: And then you got the word.

ANNA: How'd you know all this?

WESLEY: The usual route: Mary Lou to Jude to me.

ANNA: I was the one to be removed! Plus, it had to happen before I started showing. I had to leave at Christmas. Three weeks' notice. I could write my mid-terms, then out. And furthermore, I was responsible for the sanctity of my locker.

            (Pause.) I waited until everyone was in class, then I went back upstairs. I put on my gloves, I removed the safes, I scrubbed the locker, went to the can, and I was sick. I cried. I locked myself in a cubicle and cried my guts out. Then I dried my tears, threw out the gloves, went back and got a late slip from that Tomlinson goof, and I marched into class.

WESLEY: It's so unfair they made you leave.

ANNA: I doubt I could've taken another six months of that crap. I'm honestly not tough enough.

WESLEY: We're a union of two on that. *(Pause.)* I thought of you as Pincushion too.

ANNA: Do you now?

WESLEY: Of course not. But I sure did then.

ANNA: Why should you have been any different?

WESLEY: I should've known better.

ANNA: Ah, it's ancient history now. It's funny how much I still care though. God, half an hour ago, I stomped out of here and all you'd said was—

WESLEY: I'd said too much. *(Pause.)* It was Billy who stuffed your locker.

ANNA: That's no surprise.

WESLEY: I overheard him tell Jude. The night before. Jude didn't agree but she didn't try to stop him. I didn't think it was right either, but mostly I was grateful that for once they weren't doing anything to me. We're a very imperfect species. *(Holds up the bottle.)* A little more?

ANNA: Oh I'd better go.

WESLEY: No. That is, unless you want to.

ANNA: I'd like to stay –

WESLEY: You shouldn't let me drink alone.

ANNA: Half a glass then. *(As WESLEY pours.)* A bit more than that, chintzbag.

WESLEY: You said half.

ANNA: I like my halves closer to full. Shoot me a digestive. If I throw back enough of this hooch it may drown out my son the human chain saw. Maybe I'll fall asleep quickly for a change.

WESLEY: I count sheep.

ANNA: Never worked for me.

WESLEY: I count sheep, then I recite the prime ministers in chronological order. I have a big map of Canada beside my bed—it stretches across the entire wall – and I look at it and mentally drive across the country.

ANNA: Which province do you sleep in?

WESLEY: Huh?

ANNA: If the map stretches the length of your bed—

WESLEY: Oh, Nova Scotia. I lay my head just outside Halifax.
               I tried sleeping under Vancouver but I kept getting
               these bizarre dreams. *(Pause.)* If the map thing
               doesn't work, I just lie there and watch the moon. I
               love it when the moon's full and a cloud passes in
               front of it. *(Smile.)* I lie back and howl. Some nights
               I put myself to sleep thinking about suicide. About
               how I'd do it and who'd find me and after how
               long, then how the world will take the news. Will I
               get a little notice in The Examiner, will the
               neighbours have a wake—they'd better after all the
               raffle tickets their kids have sold me.

ANNA: What a sad way to make yourself fall asleep.

WESLEY: Oh, I'd never do it, don't get me wrong. It's just a
               device.

ANNA: Next time you're compiling the list of mourners,
               add me.

WESLEY: You'll come?

ANNA: I'll even help Jude with the arrangements. I'll lay in
               the sherry and the memorial digestives.

WESLEY: Spare no expense.

ANNA: Jason can pass food. We can have a short homily
               from Mary Lou Slutbrain Winters. But Wes: poor
               Mr. Bloom will want to know why.

WESLEY: Tell him the truth. "Sir, it was the waterbed. It was
               an emotional albatross." *(Pause.)* I'm glad you
               came tonight.

ANNA: I did consider going to Nutty Normans. Something

kind of drew me here. Kismet maybe. Wes. Tell me
if I'm out of line. *(Pause.)* I saw the assembly.

WESLEY: I wondered when that would come up.

ANNA: I've thought of it, of you, actually, through the
                   years.

WESLEY: *(Starting to close up shop.)* I've never talked to
                   anyone about it.

ANNA: Not even Jude?

WESLEY: Never.

ANNA: Not even the day it happened?

WESLEY: Jude came home late that night and went to bed
                   without speaking to me. I was waiting up, praying
                   to God she'd knock on my door and tell me it
                   wasn't as bad—as bad as I knew it was. She didn't
                   knock. The next day it was too late. I'd lain awake
                   all night wondering what the hell I could do to save
                   myself and, by the time dawn rolled around, I
                   knew I couldn't go back to school. Ever. I was done.
                   Kaputski.

ANNA: Why did you do it?!

WESLEY: They promised me I could join the Cougars Club.

ANNA: Who—Billy?

WESLEY: All of them. They said if I did my thing at the
                   Christmas assembly, nobody would blackball me.

ANNA: Why would you even want to belong to a club like
                   that?

WESLEY: Look. If someone offers you acceptance you don't
                   argue. I wanted to belong. To anything! I'd waited
                   seventeen, eighteen years for this—it was full
                   steam ahead, damn the torpedoes. They said I'd
                   knock them dead. I got my toga—it was actually a

flannelette sheet I'd smuggled past Mom that morning –and I changed in the dressing room and waited at the door to the gym. The cheerleaders were doing the skit before me; I stood in line behind them—they didn't really look at me, why would they? Then they ran out and did their thing and it was my turn. Billy got up to the mike and announced me. When he said he'd located the madman of ancient Rome, the Love God of Grade Thirteen Latin—I knew.

ANNA: It was a set-up.

WESLEY: And I'd fallen for it.

ANNA: Why did you go out!

WESLEY: It was too late—I had no choice!

ANNA: I remember how quiet it got.

WESLEY: It's always like that before a sacrifice.

ANNA: You looked so scared. And your arms were so white—

WESLEY: My legs were trembling so much it was like walking on sticks of Jell-O. I went over to the mike and unscrewed it. That was some feat with my hand going like this. (Shows hand shaking.) And then I started. (Recites:)

"The skies are painted with unnumbered sparks,
They are all fire, and every one doth shine;
But there's but one in all doth hold his place.
So in the world: 'tis furnished well with men,
And men are flesh and blood…"

I've run it through my head a million times. But this is where it started. Just a few at first.

"Yet in the number I do know but one

That unassailable holds on his rank..."

They were chanting by now.

ANNA: Why didn't you stop!

WESLEY: I should've but I thought... I don't know, I thought
that maybe when I did the death part, when I died,
that would satisfy them, maybe all they wanted
was some histrionics.
"Doth not Brutus bootless kneel?
Speak hands for me!"

(Mimes being stabbed.) I was drowned out by now,
even with the mike. It was coming from every
corner of that gym—from the front row of the
bleachers where the seniors were, right up to the
rafters, way back, from the younger grades and
from the ones peering in from the hall—they were
all shouting, it was hate, Anna, it had to have been,
and I was like a lightning rod for it. I stood there
and attracted hate and, when I fell to the floor, it
was like a mighty wave, a mighty wave of ridicule
that washed over me, all those voices, a thousand
people yelling "Weirdley, Weirdley". Weirdley.
My label. The name I'd been called right from the
first day I'd set foot in that school and the name I
thought I was going to leave behind that afternoon.
(Pause.) I lay there on the gym floor in front of them
all—I wanted to die—I wanted to die right then
and there—

ANNA: *(Touching him.)* Wesley—

WESLEY: *(Accepts touch.)* I'm OK. *(Pause.)* I wasn't sure the
legs were even going to get me up and out of there,
but they did, I managed to stumble away. I ran
home, it was like I could hear the chanting all the
way back, right into the house. It followed me
upstairs, up into my room and I couldn't shut it out

	until I'd crawled into bed and pulled my pillow over my head. Then, finally, it started going away.
ANNA:	I yelled it too.
WESLEY:	*(Smiling.)* Et tu Brute? Of course you did. Why wouldn't you have?
ANNA:	Pincushion, of all people, should've known better.
WESLEY:	You were only one voice in a thousand.
ANNA:	You can forgive me?
WESLEY:	Of course.
ANNA:	Can you forgive them?
WESLEY:	I pretty much have to.
ANNA:	Where do you suppose it all stops?
WESLEY:	The name-calling? I doubt it ever does. It gets subtler with adults.
ANNA:	Or maybe we just pass it down to the next generation. I meant to get down here at nine tonight. Ten at the latest. But Jason was hanging about the apartment after supper and then he dragged off to bed early. I knew something was bugging him. I went and sat on his bed and asked him. He tried to be the big tough guy for a minute but I kept on his case and finally he burst into tears. He let me hug him—he never lets me do that anymore—and then he told me the kids at school are making fun of him for never having had a father. They're calling him "bastard".
WESLEY:	They actually still use that word?
ANNA:	Apparently.
WESLEY:	I think I'd rather be called bastard than Weirdley.

ANNA: Tell that to Jason.

WESLEY: I guess Weirdley would sound pretty good to him
             right now.

ANNA: He's tough. It'll blow over. I just hope he never
             comes to hate me for it.

WESLEY: You're tough. It'll blow over.

ANNA: I hope so. *(Pause.)* The bed.

WESLEY: It's yours. Fifty percent off.

             ANNA gives a triumphant cheer.

             It'll be delivered tomorrow.

ANNA: I could squeeze it in the car.

WESLEY: Not the mattress. And you can't drive around town
             at midnight with a mattress tied to your roof.

ANNA: People might get the wrong impression.

WESLEY: *(Mock announcing.)* Pincushion makes house calls!

ANNA: Why don't I come back tomorrow and we'll load it
             then. I'll bring Jason—you can meet him. Though
             maybe I shouldn't let him see this waterbed.

WESLEY: There's still a bit of sherry left, I think.

             Produces a full bottle.

ANNA: If I have any more of that stuff I'm liable to start
             buying art.

WESLEY: "Stag in a Glen"?

ANNA: Anything, so long as it's on velvet.

WESLEY: Protestant.

ANNA: I could use something for my office, wherever
             that'll be. God. That's a whole other hassle.

WESLEY: After tomorrow you can have this place.

ANNA: I'm leaning towards a mall, if you want the dirty truth. I could run a regular practice by day and, on Thursday evenings, have a clinic. For kids. They hang out there. It's the teenage girls I worry about. They need someone to tell them their rights—who better than me?

WESLEY: You really are something.

ANNA: You can say that because you haven't seen enough of me yet. *(Pause.)* So. What about you?

WESLEY: What about me? Who knows. You need a receptionist?

ANNA: You must have some idea what you're going to do.

WESLEY: Not the foggiest. I never had to think much about the future. I didn't expect to be here forever—I knew this wasn't permanent. But the future? Anna: in just a few hours I'm starting something new. The day after tomorrow I'll wake up and look at the map beside my bed and know that I don't have to drive across Canada just in my mind anymore. I can do it for real. And I can take as long as I damn well want. Or I can stay home and do nothing. Or go out and look for a job. Am I ready for the future? Of course not, who ever is. But—but I think that maybe for the first time in my life—I'm going to toss the cat a doughnut.

ANNA: I beg your pardon.

WESLEY: Go with the flow, to use your expression.

ANNA: You may wash up in some funny places.

WESLEY: Not me—I don't flow nowhere fast.

ANNA: *(Pause.)* You may fall in love.

WESLEY: It's an option.

ANNA: Some call it an imperative.

WESLEY: Not when it's never happened. I sell the catalysts of
             love—that's as close as I get.

ANNA: But you've dated.

WESLEY: Poorly. The woman who worked here in
             Accounting asked me out on a picnic and I took
             folding chairs… There've been others—they just
             don't work out. I've never—I've never been in
             love. Never. *(Pause.)* What's it like?!

ANNA: Terrifying.

WESLEY: Really?

ANNA: It's like taking a long deep breath and suddenly
             you know you can't stop inhaling. You kind of
             want to stop and you kind of don't, but it doesn't
             matter anyway because you can't—you keep
             inhaling, you think you're going to burst and you
             just keep getting bigger and bigger and bigger—

WESLEY: I'm so sick of being lonely!

ANNA: Good.

WESLEY: I want to—

ANNA: You will.

WESLEY: You think?

ANNA: You know how you were talking about how every
             winter there's just one narrow path to your door?
             (Beat.) Things may change next winter.

WESLEY: How's that?

ANNA: One day you may look out your bedroom window
             and see a woman walking up that path.

WESLEY: My sister.

ANNA: No.

WESLEY: An Avon lady wasting her time?

ANNA: It's night. It's a woman about your age, nicely dressed, a little brassy on the outside—

WESLEY: Is this theoretical?

ANNA: *(Getting courage.)* You're upstairs. You think there's a mistake or something, maybe the woman was an apparition, so you go back to bed. However, the woman has very definitely arrived at your side door. She walks in—I guess you forgot to lock up—

WESLEY: I never forget to lock up—

ANNA: You did tonight! You hear the door slam and then she stamps her feet on the kitchen mat.

WESLEY: Do you mind if she leaves her shoes in the sun porch?

ANNA: It's too cold for that. And she's in a bit of a hurry because even though she's a modern woman—a woman of the '90s almost—she's losing her nerve. Fast.

WESLEY: Would it help her if the lights were left on?

ANNA: Just the hall one.

WESLEY: There's a night light at the top of the stairs.

ANNA: Perfect.

WESLEY: What if I'm at the head of the staircase, challenging this intruder?

ANNA: Not tonight. Tonight you're going with the flow.

WESLEY: I'm scared then.

ANNA: This woman walks up the stairs—do they creak?

WESLEY: Like crazy.

ANNA: She creaks up the stairs and goes straight to your
            bedroom.

WESLEY: There's four doors to choose from. How'd she
            know the right room?

ANNA: It's the one with the map. She walks into the
            bedroom and, for one moment, you see her
            silhouetted in the faint glow of your nightlight.
            Perhaps a stray bit of moonlight plays across her
            face.

WESLEY: I think she'd be beautiful in moonlight.

ANNA: She takes off her coat and her shoes, then
            everything else. She walks quickly over the cold
            linoleum—am I right, it's linoleum?

            WESLEY nods.

            She walks over to where you're lying on your bed,
            with your head under Halifax, and your toes
            sticking up near Vancouver, and…

WESLEY: And what? What does she do?

ANNA: She drops in on Winnipeg.

            ANNA and WESLEY both laugh.

            (Mock shock.) What a pincushion!

WESLEY: *(Pause.)* Who in her right mind would want to visit
            Winnipeg in the dead of winter?

ANNA: You'd be surprised.

WESLEY: I can't believe this.

ANNA: It comes from tossing cats doughnuts.

WESLEY: *(Pause.)* Anna. I have to close up. I have to make sure Mr. Bloom put the cash in the right place and then I have to set the burglar alarms and if I'm really brave I'll go check and make sure nobody's hiding out in the basement. You can't mess around with theory forever, not when you have a store to close.

ANNA: I was afraid not.

WESLEY: You have to be practical.

ANNA: I guess.

WESLEY: And what would be most practical is if we went back to our respective homes and got ourselves good nights' sleeps. Really good sleeps. In fact, I suggest you sleep in as late as you can. Tomorrow, treat yourself to a day on the town. Don't paint or wallpaper. Hang out at a shopping mall with Jason. Take him for a hamburger. Have a candlelight dinner at home with your Mom.

ANNA: Thanks for the thrilling itinerary.

WESLEY: I'm not finished. After dinner, watch some TV with Jason. Put on a nice dress. Your best dress, actually, then cool your heels until 9:30.

ANNA: And then?

WESLEY: And then get in your car and drive down to Bloom's Furniture. There's going to be a party.

ANNA: A real party?

WESLEY: You can't party in theory. And sometimes it's— it's—sometimes it's nice to have a date.

ANNA: Sometimes it's nice to be one.

WESLEY: After that…

ANNA: After that?

WESLEY: I don't know what happens.

ANNA: I guess we go with the flow.

WESLEY: It'll be a slow flow.

ANNA: Maybe like taking a long deep breath and never knowing where it'll end.

WESLEY: Yes. That's exactly what it'll be like.

Lights fade to black.

The End

Writing With Our Feet

for Jan Carley

Thanks

I am indebted to a great number of individuals and institutions for their help in bringing this script to maturity. Thanks first of all to Robert Garfat, who directed the Dark Horse Theatre workshop, and to its participants, Nicole Robert and Don Thompson. I'm grateful also to Theatre Terra Nova's Chris McHarge and Kevin Land, and to the original cast: Suzanne Bélanger and Nigel Hamer. Thanks also to Lesley Ewen, Ellen Rae Hennessey, Tanja Jacobs, Annie Kidder, Jackie Maxwell, Patricia Ney, Stephen Ouimette and Allan Zinyk.

The help of the Canada Council, Carnegie-Mellon Drama Showcase of New Plays, Dark Horse Theatre, Department of External Affairs, Factory Theatre, Ontario Arts Council, Shaw Festival and Theatre Terra Nova is also gratefully acknowledged.

Special thanks to Pierre Péloquin.

Production Information

Writing With Our Feet was first produced as a one-act play—consisting of about the first twenty minutes of the full-length work—at Alberta Theatre Projects' playRites 90 Festival. It was part of January's Brief New Works showcase series. It was later given a staged reading by New York City's Theatre North Collective in March, 1990, and then a full production by that same theatre, in June 1990.

Writing With Our Feet—in its full-length form—was workshopped by Vancouver's Dark Horse Theatre in April 1990, and given a staged reading as part of the New Play Centre's SpringRites Festival. Participants in the workshop were Don Thompson and Nicole Robert. Robert Garfat, Artistic Director of Dark Horse, directed. In June, 1990, the play was given a reading at the Shaw Festival, Niagara-on the-Lake, Ontario.

On October 12, 1990, the full-length version of *Writing With Our Feet* opened at Hamilton's Theatre Terra Nova, with the following cast:

JEAN-FRANÇOIS: Nigel Hamer
SOPHIE, etc.: Suzanne Bélanger

Directed by Kevin Land
Set Design by Michael Adkins
Lighting Design and Dramaturge—Christopher McHarge
Stage Manager—Barb Wright

Characters

Jean-François, Sophie, Aunt Zénaïde, Alphonsinette, Lucy Cormier, Father Rocky and Raymond Loewy.

Time

About now, or soon, and in the past, mostly after the death of JF's parents and the recent death of his sister Sophie.

Place

Ostensibly a garage underneath an access ramp in Montreal.

Dedication

My sister and I really did learn how to write with our feet. It was 1964 and the recent, unexpected death of a President was weighing heavily on our minds. If Kennedy could be bumped off so easily, what horrors awaited two youngsters living in Camelot's northernmost suburbs? At the very least: the loss of our hands. We were not impressed by our school insurance forms, which promised us a windfall $500 for each off-lopped extremity. We knew this wouldn't be enough. We knew we had to develop competent back-up systems. The entire neighbourhood could play at being outdoors children, but my sister and I huddled in the dark, practising our toes for an inevitable physiological Armageddon.

Nearly three decades have passed.

Neither my sister nor I have yet to lose a body part.

I'm beginning to think that footwriting in a darkened room while the rest of the world romps in the sun is some kind of metaphor.

Jean-François, my footwriting hero, eventually realizes his feet are best used for walking out into the world. My sister and I? We gave up footwriting and went into theatre. My sister found theatre first, but then again she was always a much better footwriter. This play is dedicated to her.

Writing With Our Feet

JEAN-FRANÇOIS (JF) is in the garage, writing. He's wearing black. At the very least, he has pinned a black ribbon to his shirt or jacket.

JF: Sophie and I were eight and ten when we began writing with our feet. Our tender minds had been deeply affected by the tragedy of our cousin Alphonsinette. After passing a long evening in disreputable company at the Arthabaska Hotel, she stretched herself across an abandoned rail-line and slid into deep sleep.

SOPHIE: *(Entering.)* Daddy's on the phone to Arthabaska! A rare train came and clipped off the legs of Alphonsinette!

JF: What!

SOPHIE: Her God-given legs! It's a one-in-a-million tragedy!

JF: Cousin Alph moved to Montreal and settled into the big wingchair in the front room. She sat there and waited for her new legs to be made.

SOPHIE: Today's quote: "I drank to forget, now look what I've got to remember: a goddamn waist that ends in mid-air!"

JF and SOPHIE laugh.

JF: She crabbed for the three months it took a master carver from St. Jean-Port-Joli to do the legs. In the meantime, Maman dug up our old baby carriage and Papa cut off the sides and the canopy. So it'd look less like a pram and more like something you'd push an angry, legless, twenty-three year-old cousin in. The carriage worked so well, and Sophie and I were such obliging pilots, that when the wooden legs finally arrived, Alphonsinette rejected them on a technicality.

SOPHIE: *(Quoting.)* "I don't like the finish. And all this carving down the side! I'll look like a goddamn souvenir!"

JF: She said that?

SOPHIE: *(Quoting.)* "First Yank tourist to see me'll rip them off. My legs'll end up on some mantelpiece in Pittsburgh! Send them back!"

JF: Daddy must be berserk!

SOPHIE: *(Quoting.)* She's lazy! I'm showing her the golden toe!

JF: And Papa did indeed give Alphonsinette the boot, forcing the government to assume her care. They bought her a wheelchair with a converted Evinrude and, today, decades later, she's a familiar sight along Rue St. Laurent, buzzing from bar to bar, sounding like a thirsty fishing boat.

SOPHIE: We can learn from this, Jean-François.

JF: How!

SOPHIE: Alphie lost her legs to teach us the big lesson.

JF: Sophie believed that horrible events occurred to warn the as-yet unscathed. Even at eight, my sister was on the cutting edge of a dark theology.

SOPHIE: Look at her! Angry! A pillow of a woman! She zigzags along St. Laurent like a drunken water beetle. Trying to forget what's vanished. Completely unprepared for life's vagaries!

JF: What's your point?

SOPHIE: What if we lost a limb or two? What if we lost our hands! We can't lose our legs because of the law of averages, not when two legs are already missing from the family tree.

JF and SOPHIE regard their hands.

But these—the innocent hands of the child.

JF: Fodder for fate.

SOPHIE: Can you imagine the horror?

JF: But how!

SOPHIE: Not a train—the family law of averages is against it. But a bloody encounter with an overturned lawnmower during a three-legged race! That'd do it!

JF: Or Papa, deranged by drink, attacking us with a machete as we sleep with arms upraised.

SOPHIE: Oh J-F, we've got to get competent back-up systems! What if Alphonsinette had taught herself to walk with her hands? At the very worst she could be doing bar-counter handstands for drink money! As for you and me...we'll learn to write—with our feet!

JF and SOPHIE regard their feet.

JF: Recognizing the wisdom of my sister's words, we set out on a program of foot-training, showing such determination, that the story of Sophie and myself is, in effect, the history of footwriting in the Americas.

SOPHIE: I'm going to use a typewriter—

JF: And this garage—this was our stage—

SOPHIE: God may take away our hands, but surely he'll leave us electricity.

JF: In no time at all, Sophie was up to twenty words a minute.

SOPHIE: Shit! My big toe just hit four keys at once. I was going for the L and I wrote PLOK!

JF: Eventually even the big toe hurdle was leapt, and Sophie could, with the daintiest of twitches, hit just one key at a time. Me, I let her use the typewriter and I worked up a kind of longhand. I'd hold my pen, which I wrapped with hockey tape for stickiness, between the big toe and toe two, and off I'd go.

Our pre-teen years passed. Then our teens. Then our post-teens. Sophie got faster and faster. She could pound out a letter to our Aunt Zénaïde in Arthabaska, a three-pager, in less than fifteen minutes. She even learned to fold the paper and stuff it into a foot-addressed envelope. For my part, I developed a languid script; large, because footwriting is not so economical of paper, but very lovely, a source of admiration to us both.

SOPHIE: It's artistic, JF! You've got real style! That's a gentleman's hand you've got in that foot!

JF: Eventually a dilemma presented itself, as dilemmas always do.

SOPHIE: (Groans.) Where does this lead? I can't spend the rest of my life writing letters to Arthabaskan aunties!

JF: I don't see why not!

SOPHIE: Granted, our inheritance means we don't have to work. And this garage is comfy—who can knock a life of footwriting in the shadow of this Willys Aero Ace? But surely there's more to reach for in life.

JF: Like what?

SOPHIE: I don't know. Philosophies.

JF: *(Not quite understanding.)* Ah—philosophies.

SOPHIE: I'm going to write instructional motifs with my feet. It's a different genre than Auntie letters and, though I've no wish to diminish letter-writing, this is tougher. Especially when one must project the muse through one's toes.

JF: I have to tell you the major difference between Sophie and me. Yes, we were related by blood and, yes, we shared many fears and aspirations. But nevertheless, there was a fundamental dissimilarity in our brains. *(Pause.)* I'm a generalist. I see the big picture. Vaguely, imprecisely, but I've got the whole ball of wax in my viewfinder. With Sophie, everything got narrowed to one precise point of accessible wisdom, and she'd see that point with perfect clarity. A reductivist Kahlil Gibran.

SOPHIE: I have to repeat a word.

JF: Myself, I'd repeat hundreds of them, sometimes for no other reason than I enjoyed their peculiar combinations of letters. I'd scrawl them out, add adjectives, adverbs, contractions…

SOPHIE: I hate like hell repeating a word when I'm only using thirteen of them in the first place—but when I read this you'll see the necessity, I hope.

           SOPHIE types.

JF: It embarrasses me to read my early work. Once, during an argument over something else

SOPHIE: —You're the reincarnation of Alfred, Lord Tennyson! *(Pause.)* I'm sorry, I'm sorry, I take it back.

JF: No—you're right.

SOPHIE: Tennyson was too strong. Uh—Sir Walter Scott.

JF: That's worse! Sophe, why don't you just say it! I'm bombastic and florid!

SOPHIE: People can't cope with bulk. They don't have the attention span. And you have to have endings.

JF: I could never finish a thought but I could always add another stanza. You see, if I finished something I'd have to let it be judged. That was scary, so I'd go and tackle giant historical movements and stay at them for a year or more: the history of Pittsburgh, the populist wit of Adlai Stevenson, the design eloquence of Raymond Loewy. Well, why not! I'd flex the toes and that'd be it, page after page after page.

SOPHIE: Almost done!

JF: But hers: anorexic jottings, environmentally correct in their careful use of space and paper... politically aware in their preoccupation with the big themes of our century. Sophie began just after the New Deal, mostly because that's when Papa's collection of Life magazines started. She'd reached the Sixties by the time she died.

SOPHIE: —Okay! You want to hear it? *(Performs.)* I'm dedicating this one to my Cousin Terry, the owner of this car, a man who understands exile and the enduring hatred of Family.

JF: *(Catching her in time.)* Funding bodies!

SOPHIE: Oh! My thanks to the minister des affaires culturelles, and to the estate of my parents. Instruction 343.

               "Medgar Evers
               Walking walking
               Moon shining
               Gun glinting

America's dreaming
Chews Mississippi asphalt."

(Pause.) So?

JF: I like it.

SOPHIE: What about "chews"?

JF: Bites?

SOPHIE: I thought of that, but I want the image of his face grinding into pavement.

JF: It's sad.

SOPHIE: And life is happy?

JF: It's a long poem, for you.

SOPHIE: I measured it. There's a hand dryer above the sinks and I can fit it right on the side. *(Packing up.)* It's perfect.

JF: My sister, she's dead now, she's just—gone now—that's another story and one that makes less sense than anything else I could tell you. It always falls to the living to create meaning out of what's gone before... For me, it's always come from Sophie the Reductivist, out here in this garage, from her feet...

SOPHIE: *(Kisses JF on the cheek; exiting.)* I'll be back in an hour. I'll pick up a pizza on the way home.

            SOPHIE exits.

JF: She'd finish a work, shoot out of the garage and off our property. She scattered her writings about the city, pinning them to trees, taping them to stop signs... her most famous ones were the God/Agog series. The entire message was God/Agog, but there were variations: God/Gagged. God/Gone. Good/God. She pasted these to churches and the Gazette ran a picture once of a sexton scraping

God/Agog off the front door of Christ Church
Cathedral.

Mostly she worked at the bus and plane terminals.
She knew that was where her words had their
maximum exposure, short of publication, which
she opposed on environmental grounds. People
would come to the bus terminal, or Dorval; they'd
see her motifs and, because they were so brief,
they'd carry them in their minds to wherever they
were headed—to every corner of the province or
any city of the world.

You see, we're really just two stops from anyplace
else. Dorval to Djakarta, Djakarta to Kupang,
Kupang to Dili. Two stopovers. All the way to
Timor and such a small chain along which to pass
the equally concise thought. The world can be a
giant thought-chain—and it was my sister who
discovered this.

Sophie's work—her last was the one she just did on
Medgar Evers—it's all still circling about, taped
from wall to wall, moving from terminal to
terminal, but most often just passing from mind to
mind. Tiny potent foot creations. Circling the
planet. Sophie's reductivist ideology, everywhere.

This then is the comfort I derive. My sister has died
without losing the use of her hands. You can over-
prepare. Me, I still sit here and write with my feet
because, Sophie having escaped that fate, the odds
are higher now I'll lose mine. And I'm shortening
up. As soon as I get down to a manageable length,
I'll rejuvenate that chain of words my sister began.
I'll leave here. I swear I will. (Unconvinced.) Of
course I will.

And—oh yes—to return to where it all started:
Cousin Alphonsinette. She met a lusty boy from
Arvida who says legs only get in the way. That

seems to make her happy on some level. They live above Le Vagabond Hotel and I'm told they've even found a priest who's willing to marry them.

Which proves there's salvation for us all, even if we haven't spent a lifetime preparing for the worst.

The Compassion of Aunt Zénaïde

	AUNT ZÉNAÏDE (AZ) bursts into the garage, wearing black.
AZ:	*(Off, getting closer.)* Allo allo allo!
JF:	*(To himself.)* Aunt Zénaïde.
AZ:	*(Bursting on.)* My boy, my boy, my boy! My poor benighted boy! *(Etc.)*
	AZ kisses and hugs JF and squeezes him to her ample bosom.
JF:	—And then there's the relatives
AZ:	—The agony you must be feeling!
JF:	—Cousins and uncles and demented aunts
AZ:	—Poor, poor Jean-François! An orphan! A brand-new orphan
JF:	—The oppression of blood and bosom
AZ:	—How can you hold up! How can you carry on! What prevents you from smashing your brains out in grief! When a baby dies it takes a mother's arms six months to recover, to stop feeling the ache for holding her child. How long will it take you to get over losing your maman and papa?!
JF:	For another year my ass will feel echoes of the belt.
AZ:	*(Decks him.)* Don't speak bad of the recently-dead!
JF:	It's the truth!

AZ:	*(Decks him again.)* I don't care! Beating is our heritage! *(Pressing JF back against her.)* Your papa beat you, he beat Sophie, Xenon beats me, we all beat each other. It's the family glue.
JF:	Where's Sophie?
AZ:	She ran out of the church.
JF:	Is she OK?
AZ:	How could she be, with her parents mouldering?
JF:	Did she have scotch tape on her?
AZ:	As a matter of fact, yes, she did.
JF:	She's at the bus terminal.
AZ:	*(Puzzled at that, then:)* I wish you could've come.
JF:	I've already explained why.
AZ:	And it's a perfectly good explanation. I'm not like all the other asswipe relatives. They never had a minute for your poor parents and now they turn around and say, "Where's Jean-François? What an ungrateful child not to see his own folks into the ground!" Those Pharisees. But couldn't you have sat outside in the long black car?
JF:	No.
AZ:	Of course you couldn't. *(Gathers him in again.)* It was a beautiful service. Apart from the religious stuff. The priest is a dolt. The homily was on dead birds. I tell you, they should bring back the Latin, that way you can only suspect what a pack of morons they all are. Dead birds! *(Pause.)* By the way, what does God/Agog mean?
JF:	It's an instruction.
AZ:	To who.

JF: To you, for starters.

AZ: *(Decks him.)* I don't like your tone! Anyway, if it's an instruction, it's a piss-poor one.

JF: Why do you ask?

AZ: I went up for communion and when I returned your poor sister'd taped it to the back of the pew.

JF: Did Sophie go up for communion?

AZ: No, she sat there like a stoic and when it was over she ran out and didn't say a word to any of the family. I don't blame her. Alphonsinette was drunk, of course. She had a flask on her and now she's back at Le Vagabond, getting pie-faced with that wastrel husband of mine. Well, I'm giving Xenon another hour, then I'm pulling him out of there by the hairy ear. The car needs gassing. We won't stay over. *(Over JF's insincere protests.)* I can't sleep unless I'm in my Arthabaska bed. *(Smothers JF again.)* You poor thing. You're not equipped for life. *(Cunning pause.)* Was there an estate?

JF: —Mmmmmnnnnnpppphhhh

AZ: A big one, a small one, an in-between one?

JF: —Mmmmmnnnnnpppphhhh

AZ: I suppose your mother brought something to the marriage but my brother was as useless as tits on a brass monkey.

JF: —Mmmmmnnnnnpppphhhh

AZ: Sophie can go out and work. She types such beautiful letters to me; she could go work for a solicitor, maybe even an English one.

JF: *(Coming up for air.)* We'll be fine.

AZ: So there is money!

JF: Enough.

AZ: I'm so—relieved. For you. *(Pulling him back.)* You could move to Arthabaska and live with us. I'll only offer once. You remember our house. We could fix up the garage just like this and even move that Willys Aero Ace back with you. Why you've kept it all these years is an incomprehension. Why that ass Terry bought it in the first place—I don't know the answer to that, either. In 1955 they built just six thousand of these and any fool would've known the car was going the way of the Dodo. Everyone else buys a Chev in 1955 except our Terry—no, he has to be different. And that's not the only way he varied from the norm.

JF: We'll stay here.

AZ: I won't offer twice.

JF: Thanks anyway.

AZ: It's your choice. I could use the company. All I do in Arthabaska anymore is sit and think. Xenon doesn't talk much and when he does say something it isn't worth hearing. You and Sophie are educated... but if you won't come you won't come. I'm not like the rest of the family, I don't belabour a point. Ah, your Papa, he was a good man. Don't ever forget that. Sure he had a temper, but that's genetic. Nothing you can do about genetics.

          But to die the way your folks died, ah, it tears out my heart. I don't give two hoots about your maman, she made him move here and I can't forgive her that. My favourite brother forced to move to Montreal, where he's a stinking fish out of water. And I curse Bombardier. I curse the day the first skidoo rolled off the assembly line. That they should all die in such a collective manner. Ten

Skidoos. Ten couples. All plunging simultaneously through the ice of Lac Aylmer. And not one of the wives sitting behind her stinking husband. Because they were swapping eh.

JF groans.

You knew they were swapping.

JF: Yes, yes—

AZ: The philistine relatives talked of nothing else, all through the holy service. No doubt the swapping was the idea of your maman. Urban slut. And for them to get fished out of Lac Aylmer after a week. Twenty corpses frozen like human ice cubes. And for them to be shoved into those cheap plywood coffins because the funeral home ran out of good ones.

JF is getting radically bugged.

And then to be driving back to Montreal and have the hearse hit that propane truck. And both vehicles blow sky high. And then to discover that just before the accident the back door of the hearse had fallen open. And your boxed parents had shot out and landed in a frozen ditch. Where they skidded through the dead bulrushes. And, unlike Moses, no Pharaoh's daughter happens along to save them.

JF is about to burst.

Oh no, it has to be a pack of hungry, thrill-seeking dogs!

JF: WOULD YOU SHUT YOUR FUCKING MOUTH!

AZ: I'm so glad to hear you say that! Already you're getting your spark back and your parents aren't even in the ground! They hadn't dug the hole yet— had I told you that? Because of the strike. So we had to leave your maman and papa lying there. *(Holds nose.)* Phew.

JF: I'LL HIT YOU INTO THE MIDDLE OF NEXT WEEK!

AZ: Spoken like your papa! This is a good sign! *(Opens bag.)* Now. I've got some things for you. I've got to yank that bastard Xenon out of Le Vagabond but first: Canada's Food Guide. Follow it. The Army's 5BX Plan. Do it. You need some muscles but don't get like that pervert Terry. There are muscles and then there are "muscles". Terry's are "muscles". Here: this is a history of Laurier. Read it. He was from Arthabaska, sort of, and this will show you how far you can go in life. Remember: it was Jean Lesage upon whose knee you dandled.

JF: I remember that!

AZ: *(Decks him.)* You were one and a half! Anyway, there's a passage in here about Lesage dandling off Laurier's knee. I've marked the page. Who can say where Laurier himself dandled? But there's a definite line of succession forming.

        Finally: television. I've made a list of all the uplifting shows on TV. It's OK to give up on God but, if you do, you should watch more CBC. And nature shows. Watch those nature shows. Turtles of Costa Rica. That kind of thing. That's as good as anything a priest can tell you.

JF: I hate turtle shows.

AZ: Of course you do.

JF: They make me suicidal!

AZ: That's the whole point! You look over the edge once or twice, you don't feel so bad you're up to your waist in shit.

JF: The plot's always the same. A mother turtle scrapes across a beach and lays a thousand eggs. Cute baby turtles hatch and with a sense of urgency crawl back towards the water. But the sky starts swarming with vultures, swooping, snatching. And from the jungle, other animals emerge. Turtle-munchers. I'm to watch this in my tender state?

AZ: But one of them always makes it to water!

JF: One out of a thousand! And you can bet your sweet life it's the one turtle with a totally retrograde personality, the real scumsucker—

AZ: No! Can't you see—the one who makes it is the noble one! The Jean Lesage turtle! The Adlai Stevenson turtle!

           Crash offstage.

JF: What's that?

AZ: Sounds like that bastard Xenon! *(Yelling off.)* Hunting for booze in the kitchen of the recently-dead, are you! *(Back to JF.)* No pride on that one. I have to go. I'm glad we had this talk. I understand you better. *(At door.)* I know you don't believe and neither do I, but just to cover the bases: God bless you, Jean-François. May He grant you peace and serenity and all that.

           AZ exits. Immediate offstage hollering at Uncle Xenon, going under JF's next speech.

           You drunken bastard! You scumsucking turtlefucker! Get out of that booze! Take that! Take that! And that!

           More roaring offstage. JF may look in at them, shake his head, return and talk.

JF: The battle was joined. Aunt Zénaïde versus that

sad excuse of a man Xenon. After a while Sophie came home and laid into them both. My parents were barely dead and not even properly buried and already my kitchen was a battlefield.

But perhaps I had been touched by Lesage and maybe some kind of inspiration had, in fact, passed to me because that night I wrote the only phrases of my florid youth that had any value. While Sophie lay in her bed sobbing I wrote poems that told of my isolation and my desire to escape. Long, silent yearnings from the heart—via the foot—that sang of who I was and what I might become—if only I could begin to dream. If only I could see what was at the centre of the ball of wax. If only I could pounce on the necessary system of thought... Sophie? Sophie?

JF goes to the door, looks into the house, then comes to.

Oh Jesus, of course... I forgot... I hear a noise, I still think it's Sophie coming home. I'd listen for her to come home from Dorval or wherever she was taping up her work. They say a mother's arms can ache... Well, so can a brother's heart. Yeah, it can really ache.

The Visitation of Raymond Loewy

JF: Sophie? Sophie…

SOPHIE is at the door.

SOPHIE: They've gone. I just waved them off.

JF: About time.

SOPHIE: Xenon's drunk but he's still got to drive, naturally. Aunt Zed insists they've had no problems since they chucked the St. Christopher's medal. But when Xenon backed over the Cormier's lawn—I saw her crossing herself.

JF: How was the funeral?

SOPHIE: About what you'd expect. It's over, that's the best I can say.

JF: Aunt Zénaïde said they were all there.

SOPHIE: It was a circus. Lots of gossip. A chorus of clucking tongues. *(Leaving.)* Lucy Cormier says "hi" and Alphonsinette sends her "profuse love". Father Rocky is threatening to visit and there's a rumour Cousin Terry's heading back east in a Nash Metropolitan.

JF: You're kidding.

SOPHIE: It's just a rumour. *(At the door.)* Did you have any supper?

JF: I wasn't hungry. Can't you stay?

SOPHIE: No. Not now. I need to be alone.

JF: There's beer in the fridge—

SOPHIE: Xenon stole it all. I'm going to my room.

JF: Soph?

SOPHIE has left.

Sophie. Sophie!

SOPHIE turns, comes back into the light. She is now Raymond LOEWY.

LOEWY: Sophie? How in Hades do I resemble your sister?

LOEWY is in full light; he grooms self.

JF: *(Under breath.)* Raymond—Loewy?

LOEWY: I expected a different reception. A tentative hosanna perhaps.

JF: It is you! My God!

LOEWY: That's a bit excessive. I'd settle for a dim smile of recognition.

JF: Mr. Loewy! Mr. Loewy, sir!

LOEWY: Too effusive! You're sounding like one of my most junior designers. Find a balance.

Warm continental greeting.

Raymond to you. Always, Raymond.

JF: I've wanted to meet you ever since, since I held my first Coke bottle, since I lit my first

LOEWY: *(Offering.)*—Cigarette?

JF: Luckies?

LOEWY: Just the packet. I fill it with Ultra Milds now, but I keep my packet, for appearances. It's not the end of the world if appearances deceive. Particularly with cigarettes.

JF: And it's a beautiful packet.

LOEWY: *(Clears throat disapprovingly.)* "Beautiful"?

JF: Effective?

LOEWY: That's a bit better.

JF: Essential form reduced to elegance.

             LOEWY lights JF's cigarette, then his own. JF draws on his cigarette. LOEWY watches carefully.

LOEWY: No no! Smoke it like this! *(Exhales continentally.)* You're holding on to it like you're from Pittsburgh! And when you stand, turn your right foot out a bit. Pose.

JF: We're in my garage!

LOEWY: Personal design transcends interiors. That might be wise. Write it down, later. And not with your foot. *(Of car.)* I can no longer ignore this.

JF: It's a Willys Aero Ace.

LOEWY: I know. 1955. What's it doing here.

JF: It's my cousin Terry's.

LOEWY: It's a monstrosity.

JF: *(Starting to imitate LOEWY, with intermittent success.)* So's Terry. He had to flee the province, and he ditched the car with us. He lives in Hollywood now.

LOEWY: Are you wondering why I'm here?

JF: A little, yes.

LOEWY: I sensed you were in trouble. That you were foundering.

             JF starts to disagree.

	My son. My I ask you a question? With whom do you speak in the course of the long, long day?
JF:	Hardly anybody.
LOEWY:	I was afraid of that.
JF:	Just Aunt Zénaïde and Uncle Xenon. They phone. And Madame Cormier from across the street looks in, though I try to discourage her. The Korean sends his son around with the groceries. People knock on my door selling causes—
LOEWY:	—I have some advice for you but, first, an historical rationale. I am Parisian by birth. I came to America when I was 26
JF:	—I know. You had a quarter in your pocket when you came and by the time you'd died you had houses in Manhattan, on the Riviera
LOEWY:	—When I arrived here I was still young enough that I could graft New World vigour to my aesthetic preconceptions. (Grimacing.) Oh, that Aero-Ace. It was style suicide. I warned them! "It's half Ford, half Hudson!" You can meld influences and achieve beauty but you can also end up wallowing in a slough of inconsequence. It's a common enough crime. Some entire nations do it.
JF:	That's not fair!
LOEWY:	Pardon?
JF:	Sir.
LOEWY:	I'm thinking of Belgium. Aren't you?
JF:	Oh. Yeah. Yeah, Belgium's pretty dismal.
LOEWY:	This Cousin Terry—is he in the movies?
JF:	Parts of him.
LOEWY:	That explains so much.

Car horn, off.

That's Mrs. Loewy, she's tired and fractious. *(Leaving, turns.)* I'm worried about you. I'm a man of infinite ego, so I can only say this once. You are my last disciple. You alone on this woebegone continent have kept the faith. My work has been bastardized beyond redemption. My bullet-nose cars are centrepieces in fern bars. There's graffiti in the lobby of the Lever Building. My Brazilian city is covered by the soot of a dying Amazon. I am dead! I can't fight back by creating anymore. There are no more Studebakers in my future, no more non-rusting refrigerator shelves...

Car horn, impatient.

You have always loved my work and you've devoted part of your life to its study. I'm honoured. But even the best-read disciple must go forth and spread the gospel sooner or later, don't you think?

JF looks away.

There is something inside you, struggling to— emerge...

Car horn, insistent.

And there is something else wanting to kill it. Who will win this little donnybrook?

Horn.

This is no good. That woman will wake the dead. We'll stop by on our way back.

Leaving; turns, throws Lucky Strike pack to JF.

Goodbye my Jean-François. Smoke in style, heh?

LOEWY exits.

A Man's Home

JF is alone on stage.

JF: "Something in me—struggling to emerge."
       Emerge emerge emerge. Emerge from where!?
       Nobody has any respect for the garage academic.
       (Chomping about.) What about study? What about
       the ivory tower? Ivory—garage. *(Stops; this might
       be worth writing down; he goes to chair.)* See, I just
       thought of that. *(Writing with foot.)* "The Ivory
       Garage." A poem by—a longish poem by Jean-
       François. *(Writes.)* As the lemming flees to sea.
       (Correction.) Hotfoots to sea. *(Mumbling.)* No, it's
       cold up there. Cold-foots. Hiphops. Showshoes.
       (Thinking about writing.) All change is like an
       iceberg. All thought is like an iceberg. So very
       much submerged. Emerged. Argh. Submerged.
       Only one-tenth...a ninth? A ninth or a tenth—only
       a portion glints in the cold sunlight and...and...
       (Crumples up sheet quietly.) Fuck.

       (Picks up hubcap.) Well my little foundling. We're
       having another uninspired day.

       When the access ramp was built over our gully it
       wasn't one day before these things began raining
       down on our house. Maman was having her beer in
       the deck chair and she nearly got beaned by the
       first one, a Pontiac. Cool as a cucumber, she turns it
       over—*(Continentally.)* et voila: ashtray.

       But the hubcaps—they land on the roof and skid
       off our eaves; they bang on to here and saucer out
       to the street. Sophie used to run out and grab them
       before the Cormiers did—Madame Cormier's a

collector, too. It wasn't long before we had all the ashtrays we needed—one for every table and chair arm—so now I hang them here.

The last time I was out the front door, all the way out, I was chasing a Plymouth. I heard it rolling across the roof and I could see the witch Cormier throwing on her coat, so I ran out fast. I didn't even think about being outside; I certainly didn't think about propping the door open.

I chased it down the street—only three houses, but I was out of breath; I hadn't started the 5BX at this point. Cormier's hot on my heels but I get there first, I grab it and then I remember how far away I am. I look back—big mistake—and there's the house and the garage—it's like they're on another planet. I'd never really seen how this place huddles under the access ramp...

I'm nauseous, faint...a white roar is jamming my skull. I walk, one foot in front of the other, not running, just walking, trying to be calm, past the Martin's, then the Rheaume's, then Monsieur Péloquin's, then across our lawn, up the stoop and just as I reach my front door *(Makes noise.)* it blows shut.

I smash at it with my shoulder but it's stubborn to me, it won't give way. "You're doomed!" Madame Cormier is crowing, rejoicing in my terror. There's one basement window and I kick at it. I kick out the divider strip and some of the glass and then I dive through. I hurl myself through—glass gouges at my back and my shoulders, it rips my scalp in long, vicious licks...but I'm inside. I'm inside, again. Safe.

Cormier peered in at me. She had the hubcap. She wouldn't go away until I swore at her.

SOPHIE: *(Offstage, warning.)* Alphonsinette!

JF: Huh? *(Back to story.)* That was the last time I was
            out. Now, whenever I see hubcaps rolling down
            the street I remind myself I've got enough. Cormier
            can help herself.

SOPHIE: *(Offstage, warning.)* Alphonsinette!

JF: Christ, Alphonsinette. *(Back to story.)* Anyway, this
            is a roundabout way of saying there aren't many
            advantages to living in the shade of an access
            ramp. No one even knows what it's giving access
            to! It's the same one Cousin Terry escaped on—
            maybe it leads to Hollywood. *(Shrugs
            continentally.)*

SOPHIE: *(Offstage.)* Alphonsinette's coming!

            Growing sound of Evinrude outboard.

JF: *(Pulling paper up; footwriting.)* "Concerning hubcap
            avarice: Propelled by it, he took many risks, many
            times leaving his flanks exposed—

SOPHIE: *(Offstage.)* She's at the driveway! I'm hiding!

JF: "But his passion for dulling chrome, the flotsam of
            accessing vehicles, blinded him to the tearing
            hunks of his soul."

Alphonsinette's Brilliant Scheme

Alphonsinette (A) roars into the garage on her motorized wheelchair. It has an Evinrude outboard mounted on the back for propulsion; the front may have a Studebaker bullet nose.

A: Great stuff JF! Powerful! It's a strong argument for feet! God, were you smart to stay away from that funeral! Where's your sister?

JF: Probably downtown.

A: She's always downtown!

JF: Well, that's where she is. *(Tries to resume work.)* You could try the bus terminal.

A: Come on! This is no time to be anti-social! How often do I visit! How often do your parents have a funeral, for that matter? I'm family. Don't turn your back on family. After all, who can defend you from family—but family? And listen, I'd've come yesterday but I had to wait until that maniac Xenon was gone. *(Pause.)* And I'm truly sorry.

JF: Thanks.

A: It makes no difference to me they were Swappers. I feel their loss just as keenly. After I lost my legs, things didn't look so bright for old Alphonsinette. Maybe a job in a circus. Maybe a lecture tour of the CEGEPs, warning of the perils of drink. But your papa, my good uncle, he took me in.

JF: He also kicked you out.

A: That was my fault, and I bear him no malice. I'll never forget that before he kicked me out, he took me in.

JF: We had a good time pushing you up and down the street.

A: And the way you'd hurtle me around the corner on two wheels. Ah, those were the days. *(Cunning pause.)* Yes, those days remain a beacon of happiness to me amid the dimming light of my life.

JF: How're things at the hotel?

A: Fine, wonderful. Except they're tearing it down.

JF: —Ahh—

A: It's historical.

JF: I see.

A: It might remind people of things, if you were to leave it standing there. People approach memories in the strangest ways. Especially politicians.

        Banging noise.

        What the hell's that?

JF: Probably a hubcap. *(Gets up and peeks out.)* There it goes, off the curb. Cormier's already in hot pursuit—she's got a sixth sense for them now.

A: *(Looking.)* She can really move for an old cotton top.

JF: It's turning the corner. It'll be at the Korean's—

A: *(Feigning interest.)* Ah yeah, there it goes…I was wondering—

JF: Sophie and I are happy here, together. Thank you for offering to move in with us.

        A protests.

Whenever anyone praises my writing I know they're heading for a big request, and when you told me about your hotel... We want to live alone. Anyway, I thought you had a boyfriend from Arvida!

A: I do!

JF: Tell him to put you up!

A: I thought he could move here too. You'd like him. You're very similar. You're stuck in here and Arvida, well, he won't come out of the bedroom. Things don't look so good for us once they tear down Le Vagabond. The city's expensive now and we've only got little pensions.

JF: Big enough for beer.

A: But not enough to—ah—set us up in business.

JF: What qualifies you for business!

A: Initiative. Foresight. Creativity. Plus an idea. Hold up your finger. Come on. Give me your thumb.

        JF does. A sprays something on it from a small mouth-spray-like container, with an air of intense concentration.

JF: What're you doing! What is this! It's turning to rubber!

A: It's the idea of the century!

JF: What is it!

A: Spray-on condoms!

JF: What!

A: Think about it! What's the biggest problem facing us today! Everyone hates using condoms. We know we're supposed to—we know we have to—

but even the most inventive lover has difficulty installing the latex condom without calling for a minor intermission. And they don't feel right.

JF: How do you know?

A: My man says it's like shaking hands with a skidoo mitt over your wiener.

JF is laughing.

Come on, JF, hear me out! Answer me this: what does the modern person do best?

JF: Watch TV.

A: *(Decks him.)* Spray, dummy! Spray!

JF: —Spray, spray!

A: We spend our lives spraying ovens, lawns, hair… So picture the scene, JF. A couple in the final throes of foreplay. The man's cock is hopeful, inquisitive. The woman's pubic pasture is a dew-drenched meadow.

JF: Oh my god.

A: He asks her, "Now?" She says, "OK, my love," and reaches to her bedside table.

Sprays.

A few passes with Alphonsinette's invention and he is ready. She smiles invitingly. He says, "You spray well, my love. Not thickly like some. For example, Lucy Cormier sprays so much my dick feels like a hockey puck."

JF: Leave Lucy out of this.

A: Sorry, I was trying to be funny. My couple has wild sex, no babies, no disease, no regret… what do you think!?

JF: Wow.

A: The idea of the decade at least!

JF: It's not bad.

A: Not bad! It's a sure thing! I'll be famous! I'm already practising applications for when I go on the talk shows. *(Sprays randomly, carelessly, perhaps murmuring a variety of names.)* The slut. *(Sprays with prolonged industry.)* The fearful mother of six.

JF: Wait a minute! What happens after!

A: After?

JF: How does he get rid of it?

A: Rid of it?

JF: How do you remove a spray-on condom?

A: Turpentine.

               JF yowls.

               It's the only thing I've found that removes the rubber.

JF: You want him to roll over and stick his dick in a bowl of turpentine?!

A: It's a flaw, I admit it! We're working on solutions! We're going to hire a scientist who can figure something else. My poor Arvida man, he's all in favour of my invention. But I've made him test so many removers he's starting to lose the Big Zucchini. And no one else will volunteer to try.

JF: Don't even ask.

A: I would never endanger family.

JF: So what about those scientists? I'm told they cost money.

A: Even a third-rate one can run you a hundred a day.

JF: Ahh.

A: We don't need a lot! Just a little start-up capital. The government'll kick in as soon as we've got a few thousand raised. And we know our MP. I've got a few things on him. We'll get students on summer grants. There's an agency that helps women without legs get started in business. It'll be clear sailing once we pitch our tents. We'll be rich. We can buy Arthabaska and throw out every last one of those bastards we're related to.

           Light begins fading on A.

          You can drive around Montreal in a car with black windows—it'll be like never leaving home. You'll get better, slowly. First the black windows, then a car with tint, then you can drive, maybe a convertible, maybe that Willys, then a bike. Before long we'll have you lecturing on TV. Speaking of the new entrepreneurial spirit sweeping the province. Jean-François this, Jean-François that. A name for the Nineties. Lights, cameras, celebrity... Jean-François!

           Light is entirely off A. The light remains on JF, who is locked in an attitude of horror and wonderment, studying his thumb.

Agoraphobia

Light comes back up on Aunt Zénaïde (AZ), who is holding a bottle of pills.

AZ: You can't stay in here the rest of your life! As your senior relative, I forbid it!

JF: I'll go out when I'm ready!

AZ: But when will that blessed day be? The world isn't standing still!

JF: Let it move without me!

AZ: Even Arthabaska's shaking a bit with the times! Now brighten up! Take some responsible measures!

JF: Maybe I'll pray.

AZ: Screw that! Gobble these. *(Holds up bottle.)* Beta-blockers. *(When there's no response.)* JF! These babies top the 5BX and the Canada Food Guide by a country mile. In Arthabaska we talk of nothing else. You want out? These will open the heaviest door!

JF: I'm not interested!

AZ: Then you'll rot!

JF: I'll rot!

AZ: Rot! *(Shakes bottle, maybe pops a pill or two.)* Rot, see if your favourite aunt cares.

JF: I'm only interested in organic solutions.

AZ: Fine, rot organically. *(Pause.)* So, have you seen Alphonsinette?

JF: She comes 'round some days.

AZ: She doesn't write me, you know.

JF: Forgive me, dear Aunt, but why would she?

AZ: She's my daughter! I want to know what she's doing with her life. At the very least she could send me a thank-you note.

JF: For bad-mouthing her?

AZ: For investing.

JF: You put money into the spray?!

AZ: It's a cash cow! Xenon and I cleaned out the mattress for her. And for what? Sure, we have the satisfaction of seeing her on the talk shows. We can sit in our Arthabaska living room and bask in the reflection of her TV shadow. But when people ask, "What do you hear from that famous, legless daughter of yours?" I have no answer because she doesn't write. No, Alphonsinette thinks I'm an ogre. That's her perception. An ogre. It's not so bad out there, JF, I swear it. There's a lot of energy on the street you can't get in a garage. It might help you with your writing. Tell me there aren't substantial drawbacks to this life of yours.

JF: I never see a woman in a dress.

AZ: That's bad, yes.

JF: Madame Cormier only ever wears slacks.

AZ: Even Xenon wouldn't look at that one. The daughter, yes, but—

JF: I can't see the river. I can't smell the deep water and you can't even see the mountain from my bedroom anymore, not since the expressway got built. I only catch the sunset when it reflects off the Cormier's windows. Rainbows? The sun spangling the afternoon lake? *(Shrugs continentally.)*

AZ: This regret makes me hopeful change will follow.

JF: Nah.

AZ: Your ancient Auntie can hope, can't she?

JF: Once, not long before this started, I went with Lucy Cormier to the beach. We were still lovers then and it should've been a good afternoon. You couldn't actually swim in the water—there were signs posted. But you could lie on real sand in the company of thousands.

AZ: That's nice eh? Real sand, the river—

            AZ can be leaving.

JF: I walked along the edge of the water, taking care to not let any part of me come in contact with it. I paced off a yard and did a census of what I could make out through the murk: one natural yoghurt cup, no preservatives; one bellied-up perch; a green garbage bag waving through the water like a giant manta ray. There was a thermal inversion that day, too. The air was foul; it'd been locked over Montreal for a week. Some said it came direct from Pittsburgh.

AZ: Pittsburgh!

JF: I knew you'd appreciate that. Oh, and that day? There were three murders and six bank hold-ups, and on the bus home we saw someone dead on the road with the ambulance right there.

AZ: That's efficient

JF: —Well, yes it was, because the person had actually been killed by the ambulance as it was speeding somewhere else. And you tell me I should be getting out? You want me out in that? Here, there's the honest smell of warm dirt, the healthy sound of the cicadas outside, buzzing above the accessing traffic. Bits of sun slip through the walls there and there, wherever the boards are splitting. Paintbrushes line up like old soldiers...my hubcaps are here, and philosophy, meditation, art... *(Gestures out.)* Chaos. Fools. Disease.

Pessimism

Introducing FATHER ROCKY.

ROCKY: Even I don't say it's that bad!

JF: Father Rocky!

ROCKY: Why're you surprised?

JF: Well, after the way Sophie treated you at the hospital

ROCKY: —She was in pain. That anger—she didn't mean it for me. She's gone now; my duties lie with the living.

JF: What a lot of bullshit that is.

ROCKY: You may not know it, but you need me.

JF: Like I need the clap.

ROCKY: This defensive posture you adopt when confronted by the clergy—it hints of a torn heart.

JF: Oh Christ.

ROCKY: A heart insecurely secular.

JF: I'm not interested.

ROCKY: Your sister abused me with conviction, but you protest too much.

JF: Did Aunt Zénaïde send you?

ROCKY: God sent me.

JF: Did He get a phone call from my aunt?

ROCKY: She's worried. You're not answering your phone. She thought maybe you'd hung yourself from grief. She called me a dolt and, in the next minute, she begged me to look in on you. It's so typically ambivalent.

JF: We were the first generation to give up on the church, Sophie and me. After a thousand years of kissing the bums of every passing priest we said, "That's enough, we go it alone from here on in." And we said it on behalf of all our ancestors. We purged the church right off the tree. The skin of faith slipped away so easily, like a lizard shedding—

ROCKY: Smoke?

           ROCKY pulls out a pack of Luckies, and offers one to JF.

JF: Just one. Then you have to go.

           ROCKY and JF light their cigarettes and begin smoking. JF smokes à la Loewy.

           You do that like a peasant.

ROCKY: I am a peasant.

JF: Don't sound so proud of it. Hold it like this. Turn your right foot out. Pose. And don't look so greedy when you inhale.

ROCKY: I've lost many sheep over the years, but the loss of you and your sister has hurt me the most. Of all the sheep in my fold, you and Sophie had the greatest potential for clutching God to your breasts.

JF: Wait a sec—did I say I'd given up on God?

ROCKY: Oh?

JF: I haven't given up on God, just on your bullshit.

ROCKY: "Theory without practice is barren."

JF: Yes, and we know who said that eh.

ROCKY: Jesus Christ.

JF: *(At same time.)* Karl Marx!

             They shrug.

             Anyway, you're a fine one to talk about theory and
             practice.

ROCKY: Hold on! I've established a boxing club for young
             girls! And the province has given us permission to
             ladle soup every Thursday. They give us a
             schedule of acceptable soups and we spoon it out
             to the humble masses. Plus, I'm setting up a
             workshop for the handicapped in the church
             basement—we'll be threading rosary beads and
             mailing them to the faithful in Third World
             countries.

JF: These are reasons to show up at Mass? And don't
             try frightening me into coming, either.

ROCKY: Then I appeal to your sense of compassion.

JF: Oh please.

ROCKY: The little boxing girls don't believe. They laugh at
             me. The bums who slurp my soup are too far gone
             to care; they've witnessed too much of the
             roughness of life. I'm even losing my grip on the
             handicapped. Your Cousin Alphonsinette
             ridicules me at every turn. Her billboards
             surround my church. Evening mass is ruined by
             the flashing of her condom ads. If fear and
             practicality can't draw you back—can pity?

JF: Sophie'd kill me.

ROCKY: Sophie's dead.

JF: She'd resurrect just to kill me.

ROCKY: Resurrection's been done.

JF: I don't believe in God.

ROCKY: You just said you did.

JF: I lost it.

ROCKY: Just like that.

JF: I'm agoraphobic!

ROCKY: You can sit in the confessional!

JF: Sorry. I'll give you money for your soup kitchen.

                JF begins footwriting a cheque.

ROCKY: No one can say I didn't try.

JF: And I'll ask Alph to lay off the billboards.

ROCKY: I almost had you.

JF: I'm vulnerable right now. It would have been a false victory.

ROCKY: God doesn't care about methods! For him it would've been as noble a triumph as if I...as if I'd brought your Cousin Terry back to the straight and narrow path.

JF: Speaking of paths...

ROCKY: What.

JF: Father, what is it you do in the gully?

ROCKY: It's not a gully anymore. It's an underneath-the-access ramp.

JF: What do you do down there? It seems odd to look out my kitchen window and see a priest slipping down the gully path. And Madame Cormier says you go every day. Collecting hubcaps, are we?

ROCKY: I have a hobby.

JF: I can imagine.

ROCKY: I count dead birds.

JF: You count dead birds.

ROCKY: I count them. I give them last rites. I bury them.

JF: You don't expect me to believe that—

ROCKY: Two years ago I was sweeping the front steps of the church and a rock dove fell at my feet. Overlooking the obvious symbolism of the act, a small bell rang in my head: "hobby". After all, if God can see the little sparrow fall, the least I can do is keep a list. I wrote down 'dove' and then it occurred to me that, as a priest, I had to do more than just look. So I buried. There's plenty of people keeping track of the live birds—I'll watch over the dead ones. And there's a great diversity of them in that bastardized gully: redstarts, thrushes, thrashers—

JF: You bury birds.

ROCKY: Yes.

JF: That's pathetic.

ROCKY: Is it any more so than burying your sister? And your parents? The Swappers. We all look for meaning in this life and, yes, tending to dead flying creatures is a nearly meaningless act—but if you add it all up, if you add up the number of nearly meaningless acts I've performed over the last two years, something develops. At least for me. And it's not for you to belittle that. It certainly isn't for you to define what has or hasn't meaning. "Theory without practice"? You're as rusty as that old Willys there. You cynics make me sick.

Love

FATHER ROCKY tears off his robe in disgust.
Underneath—he's LUCY Cormier, JF's old flame.
She is wearing black, in mourning for SOPHIE.

LUCY: But there's no mountain in Toronto. A lot of wonderful gullies but no mountain. Your eyes are never pulled upwards there, just down. Not that I'll even have eyes left to see anything with. I'm losing them to the computer screen.

JF: Sophie and I never computerized.

LUCY: That's too bad. Your sister'd have found it liberating. She could've written less, more quickly. Anyway, my eyes and my back are going, my ovaries are vapourized. I never realized how truly mundane life could be until I transferred there. Toronto is a city vindicated by the VCR. The men make love like sewing machines. The only relief from boredom is fear. There's a vast parking garage under my building—it terrifies me. When I go down to my car I whistle a tune, not to sound bold, but because I figure there's a one in a million chance I'll be whistling the song that's special to my killer. Maybe the song his mother whistled to him at the breast. So he'll spare me. My apartment's a boring box, my job's tedious; all I have is the terror in between.

JF: Lucy and I'd go down in the gully. This is the same gully the expressway molested but in those days it was deep, deep enough to save the coolness of the night all day long, and dense enough to grant us the privacy to explore each other's bodies…far away from the vigilance of the street.

LUCY: It was magic.

JF: Yeah, there was magic in this ugly cul de sac.

LUCY: The best part was, it was forbidden.

JF: It drove them crazy. And we'd lie in the dirt, we'd fuck our way through that gully, from one bank to the other

LUCY: —On the culvert

JF: —Beside the culvert

LUCY: —In the dirt, against the tree, straddling the log

JF: And when we were done we'd rinse ourselves in our spit and I'd brush you dry with the flat leaves… We'd lie there for hours, just off the path.

LUCY: Ahead of me, inches from my face, there were those thin pools of sunlight marking the path, and Maman's cat would creep along and stare at us.

JF: Up on the street the car doors would thunk, but the sounds you and I made stayed a secret down there.

            They begin kissing.

LUCY: JF?

JF: Mmm?

LUCY: Let's go.

JF: Go? Go where.

LUCY: The gully. I've thought of nothing else. The whole drive down. All through your sister's mass. Let's go.

JF: Out?

LUCY:	Yes! We're in here—and the gully's out there.
	JF is demurring.
	It's the same gully JF, I'm the same Lucy, it's the same sunlight, same path—
JF:	I can't.
LUCY:	And the dirt, the sunlight
JF:	I can't go.
LUCY:	The broad flat leaves, the sun pools, me, you
JF:	No!
LUCY:	Yes!
JF:	*(Pushing LUCY away.)* I can't go out!
LUCY:	Yes you can!
JF:	I'm agoraphobic! You don't understand! I physically cannot step out. I'd choke. I'd stop breathing. I couldn't breathe.
LUCY:	I don't buy this agoraphobia shit!
JF:	It's true!
LUCY:	That's not what I think. That's not what anyone thinks. Agoraphobia? *(Sound of disgust.)*
JF:	I have a disability certificate.
LUCY:	I'm supposed to be impressed by that? I'm supposed to believe a piece of paper you got some quack to sign? Why don't you just admit it?! If you wanted to go out, you would—but you don't want to. And the reason you don't want to—is you're scared.
	JF turns away.

You're spineless. You're too fucking spineless to even bury your own sister. You're even afraid of me. Admit it! You're afraid of me!

JF: Maybe I don't want you!

LUCY: I've never loved anyone like I loved you. We've shared a lot, you and I. When you bunkered down here I couldn't bear the thought of never seeing you again, of never being with you, never being—in your arms or...I moved away, it was the only thing I could do. And now, time's passed. It's different now. This time I'm going voluntarily. Toronto isn't my first choice of places to be but it has one important advantage over here—it doesn't have you.

            LUCY exits.

JF: Wait! Wait!

            JF might run to the garage window. He may try to exit, and fail. Finally he collapses under the weight of his loss, and begins to grieve for his sister.

            Sophie. Sophie. *(etc.)*

A Bit of a Relapse, Then a Start to the Recovery

SOPHIE appears with a sheet, scissors and mirror. She'll wrap JF and start to snip at his hair.

SOPHIE: *(Wrapping him.)* Why don't you just let it grow long like Jesus?

JF: It would give Father Rocky hope.

SOPHIE: But nobody's going to see you in here.

JF: Personal design transcends interiors.

SOPHIE: That's smart—you think it up?

JF: It's from Loewy.

SOPHIE: *(Wielding scissors.)* I might have guessed. So, what's the personal design in coiffure this month? How about a brush cut!

JF: Eggheads don't look good brush-cut.

SOPHIE: You're not an egghead. You're a garage populist.

JF: Well I just want a trim. And nothing off the front. Any mail?

SOPHIE: No.

JF: Are we of no consequence to the mailers of mail?

SOPHIE: Apparently.

JF: *(Sees letter.)* But—what's that?

SOPHIE stands on it, or attempts to hide it.

	That's a letter. Who's it from?
SOPHIE:	*(Picking it up.)* No one.
	JF grabs it.
JF:	*(Sniffs.)* I can smell Old Spice. It's from Cousin Terry.
	SOPHIE grabs it back.
	Open it up!
SOPHIE:	I already did. It was addressed to me.
JF:	So read it!
SOPHIE:	It's personal.
JF:	*(Pouts.)* This is nice. The garage begins to have secrets. His sister begins concealing things from him. Is it for his own good? I think not. Information withheld never benefits anyone. *(Sighs.)* "The way of the egghead is hard."
SOPHIE:	Oh for God's sake, it's just a letter. He smashed his car.
JF:	The Nash! And you weren't going to tell me! *(Pause.)* What else did he say?
SOPHIE:	*(Pause.)* He wants me to visit.
JF:	I know.
SOPHIE:	How'd you know!
JF:	I already read the letter.
SOPHIE:	It was addressed to me!
JF:	You shouldn't have left it out.
SOPHIE:	Christ JF, it was personal.
JF:	He's a real bastard for trying to lure you out there.

SOPHIE: It's only a visit! He needs a car! That Willys is just gathering dust. I'll drive it out.

JF: You'll get mugged by a hitchhiker in Iowa and your corpse'll be cut up into little pieces and

SOPHIE: I'm taking Lucy Cormier for company. She's studying self-defence. I'm picking her up in Toronto and we're heading west.

JF: What if the car breaks down? Where are you going to find spare parts for a 1955 Willys Aero Ace?

SOPHIE: You worry too much.

JF: You really think you'll like it out there? It's awful in LA. Even Terry says that. You'll have a huge let-down. You'll be depressed for months. You'll get all the way to the coast—barring a bloody encounter with a serial killer—you'll get out there and you'll end up like Terry: disillusioned, colour-enhanced, dried-up, used-up, a crumpled human Dixie cup tossed on the side of the Hollywood Freeway.

SOPHIE: In just two weeks.

JF: *(Pause.)* You won't come back.

SOPHIE: Of course I will.

JF: Terry didn't.

SOPHIE: Terry had no choice. And he didn't have anyone to come back to. I've got someone who needs me. One way or another, I'll never leave you.

            SOPHIE has finished cutting. She hands JF the mirror and puts down the scissors.

            How's that?

JF: Very nice. A bit post-modern

SOPHIE swats him.

But very nice.

SOPHIE: I should start a salon, eh?

JF: You could learn to cut hair with your feet.

               SOPHIE is moving off, and laughing.

You'd make more money than Alphonsinette.

               SOPHIE has reached the door. JF is finding grey hair. For the first part of the following speech he'll also be trying to cut his own hair, holding the mirror etc.—it's an awkward process.

Oh oh. What's this? A prominent grise? *(Pulls it.)* Ow! *(Pulls others.)* She didn't visit Terry. I kept after her day and night and when it looked like I wasn't getting anywhere I removed some crucial parts from the Willys and mailed them off to Pittsburgh. To Terry's old address. To the city that welcomed him with smoky arms. Where he built up his muscles and girded his loins for the attack on Hollywood. Where he would flex and ungird and where he wouldn't be visited by Sophie, because she was here with me. Because I made her stay.

               JF appears to be on the verge of writing, but then he begins remembering a phone call he got from SOPHIE when she was in the hospital.

SOPHIE: You'll have to leave the garage.

JF: No!

SOPHIE: You can only sustain illusion for so long, then rot sets in.

JF: I'm not rotting.

SOPHIE: With time, fantasy loses its beauty and becomes just another foolish affectation.

JF: What do you know about fantasy?

SOPHIE: I know what it isn't. What I'm feeling—is not fantasy.

JF: *(Whispering.)* I'm sorry, Sophie.

SOPHIE: I'm not coming home.

JF: There are ways.

SOPHIE: No.

JF: Yes!

SOPHIE: You'll quickly lose your power to imagine me back.

JF: Don't say that!

SOPHIE: I have to.

JF: *(Beat.)* Does it hurt so much?

SOPHIE: Forget about that. Physical pain I can deal with. JF—listen to me! You're going to become ugly in there. Isolation—it breeds stupidity. You'll become ugly and cross with the world. March to the sea! Promise me you'll do that! JF! Oh, JF!

And JF begins to write the short poem with his feet. He begins in torment, but quickly he becomes calm.

Farewells

> *This scene includes ALPHONSINETTE (A); RAYMOND LOEWY, AUNT ZÉNAÏDE (AZ), as well as JEAN-FRANÇOIS (JF), of course. It starts out with ALPHONSINETTE roaring on stage, heavily into the Mexican motif; sombrero, castanets etc. JF snaps to.*

A: Careeemba ay yi yi *(etc.)*

JF: Oh God.

A: Careemba! Juan-Francisco, Juan-Francisco! I've come to say 'Adios amigo'!

JF: Where are you going!?

A: Acapulco—Me-hee-co. I'm moving the whole shebang down there.

JF: Why?

A: Cheap labour for starters. And the Ministry of Health is on my ass.

JF: Didn't you fix the turpentine thing?

A: Yeah, we got that solved all right.

JF: With?

A: Diet Pepsi.

JF: That's an advance?

A: Marginally. Trouble is, prolonged use of Diet Pepsi can eat away the penis, so the Feds are whipping my baby off the market. There's hypocrisy for you. The Pill causes strokes and God knows what else, but all I do is scald a few wieners and they shut me down.

JF: It seems funny, doesn't it, making millions preventing thousands, then having to move to a more benign climate. And all because a train took off your legs. It's the old amputation-opportunity thing.

A laughs and pulls JF down for a hug.

We'll see each other again.

A: I doubt it. There'll be great reluctance in certain quarters to letting me back in the country.

JF: Maybe I'll come to Mexico.

A: Whoah! Can this be my JF talking?! Well, there's a lot of hills in Acapulco, it's true. I'm going to need someone to push me around.

JF: What about your tester from Arvida?

A: He doesn't walk too good anymore. *(Hands over condom sprays.)* Here. Factory seconds, use 'em in good health.

There's a siren in the distance.

Oh oh. Time for Alphonsinette to exit. I've got Arvida idling on the access ramp. *(Kisses JF.)* If anyone asks, tell them I ran off to Pittsburgh—there's a family precedent eh?

JF: Yeah—I'll be seeing you. Before you know it, maybe.

ALPHONSINETTE turns around. She's become Raymond LOEWY. He picks up the condom spray.

LOEWY: *(Reading label.)* Le Vagabond Pharmaceuticals?

JF: My cousin owns the company.

LOEWY: She needs a designer.

JF: She was getting her bottles from a mouth spray company.

LOEWY: Every object has its ideal form.

JF: But a condom spray?

LOEWY: Think.

JF: I suppose it could glow in the dark, so you can find it on your bedside table.

LOEWY: Good.

JF: And it could have a penlight attached—so you could aim?

LOEWY: Excellent. *(Pulls out Luckies.)* You want another of these?

JF: Sure.

            LOEWY and JF smoke in great style.

LOEWY: *(A continental sigh.)* A few thoughts: Your sister was right. Simplicity is the end. That's not the same as all that "less is more" nonsense—don't get the two confused. Reduction enhances. Form should be humble. I had to inhale the art of a thousand years before I could design my Coke bottle. But JF? I'm just a designer. I'm the best designer to have ever walked this planet, but that's still no reason to make a cult of me.

JF: What would I lose by leaving here?

LOEWY: Nothing. Not a thing. Not as long as you honour the essence of you, and carry it into the future. After all, if you forget who you are, how can you understand what you might become?

Car honk.

(Continental shrug; turns to leave.) By the way. On the drive up, in central Vermont, we were passing through a rock cut and someone had spray painted "God/Agog".

JF: That's from my sister.

LOEWY: I know.

JF: *(As LOEWY is leaving.)* Raymond?!

           LOEWY half turns.

LOEWY: Mm?

JF: I'm going to tape a foot-something in the Lever Building!

           LOEWY smiles and waves continentally. He makes a full turn and now he is AUNT ZÉNAÏDE.

AZ: I see Alphonsinette the slut's been here. *(Picks up condom bottle.)* You know she's wanted for fraud heh? That spray-on rubber—it never worked. She sold a million bottles and nine months later the stinking birth rate's shot up higher than Duplessis' fondest dream. So look: are you still feetwriting?

JF: Trying.

AZ: Just because your sister's gone, doesn't mean you should stop. How come you say "trying"?

JF: People won't leave me alone.

AZ: Is that a hint? Fine, hints I take for free. I'm only here out of respect for your father's memory. Just stick my head in the foot-garage and then haul my ass back to Arthabaska. Xenon's not well. Now that I've got the upper hand he's feeling the back of it. It's been 45 years and finally, now, when I get the urge, I deck him. I've discovered there's an element of truth in violence. I've learned the secret that men know from birth. I'm empowered!

AZ is shaking her fist at JF.

So watch what you write about your old aunt!

AZ continues to shake her fist at JF, but he catches her arm, and kisses her hand.

You men. You don't fool me. *(Gently, pulls him to her.)* Write us some modern truths, boy. Get those toes in motion. Do something. Do something, or rot.

JF: *(With her.)* Or rot.

AZ releases JF and exits. JF watches her go. He remembers the phone conversation.

(On phone.) Sophie. Sophie? Are you still there?

A Decision is Made

With JEAN-FRANÇOIS and SOPHIE.

SOPHIE: Just let the front lawn grow over. It'll drive Madame Cormier nuts.

JF: I might get it paved.

SOPHIE: That's even better. Cement a hubcap or two on it—really put her under. The roof's going to need repairs in six years. I've left the name of the company in a file on my dresser. And the furnace, too—you'll have to replace it by the end of the century. The Korean will deliver your food and his boy will go the bank for you, at least until he's too busy with university. They promised.

JF: You're sounding like Aunt Zénaïde.

SOPHIE: I'm dying, and you say that?

JF: I mean, the way she was giving me orders after Maman and Papa died.

SOPHIE: You could do worse than to get out her 5BX book. Lucy tells me you're looking a bit puffy.

JF: She hasn't seen me.

SOPHIE: Madame Cormier's got a telescope now. Listen, you should be nicer to her, and when Lucy comes to see you, be nice to her, too. And, if you can, make peace with the Arthabaskans and try and get Cousin Terry to come home. He's a mess.

JF: And Father Rocky?

SOPHIE: Don't let the church within a block of your life, ever again. You can contemplate God, but don't you dare do it in the company of strangers. *(Pause.)* I could've wished you were here.

JF: Why are you saying that now!?

SOPHIE: I don't know. Sorry. Everyone else says it and I guess I'm just repeating. Forget I mentioned it. But what if Aunt Zed drove you down here and parked in the lot beneath my window... we could wave... would that be so bad?

JF: The last thing she told me before she slipped into incoherency was that she was concentrating on a chip in the enamel of her sink.

SOPHIE: It's at head level. I'm taking the chip from the larger whole and by blocking out everything that surrounds it, I'm enhancing its beauty.

JF: I was afraid that the pain she was suffering, and the smells and the noise of the hospital would be too much for her, that they'd overwhelm her capacity to reduce, but no

SOPHIE: — The chip's as beautiful, as good as a berry on the Cormier hedge or the waxwing feather Father Rocky brought me from the gully...or even the snub-nose on Raymond Loewy's prize car.

                         Light off SOPHIE.

JF: She was only 80 pounds when she died. She weighed seven at birth and I think she was trying to get back to that. Aunt Zénaïde looked after the burial. Sophie's in Notre Dame-Des-Neiges, alongside my parents. And naturally, I had her cremated. And now I've written my first short piece. It's amazing, being so reduced.

                         SOPHIE reappears. She's dead. JF hands her the poem.

SOPHIE: *(Reads it.)* It's really good. It's beautiful. *(Counting.)* You've only used four words. Poor Lord Tennyson.

JF: He's flown the coop. And now I'll be writing these.

SOPHIE: And? *(Holds up poem.)*

JF: And.

SOPHIE: And? *(Smiles, holds out poem.)*

JF: *(Taking poem from SOPHIE.)* And now I'll have to do something with it.

> *Light off SOPHIE, who is able to go now.*

In the life of every nation there's a moment of hush, a twenty minutes to the hour pause when the collective will quietens. And then swells. It's as if we're all walking with linked arms into Lac Aylmer and, just before that cold water reaches our crotches, we stop. And then, with a sigh that runs the length of our line, we settle into the lake, we immerse in the waters, right to our necks, together. And in that moment there's sadness, an awareness of pain, an acknowledgment of change. And then an inkling of joy. Am I right?

(Announcing.) To the amazement of everyone on the cul-de-sac Birch, Jean-François in the early evening of *(Today's date.)* flung open the door of his garage.

> *The garage door is opening; colour outside. JF looks out, and turns back.*

There's one last leaf on my tree. It's coloured. All its brother and sister leaves have preceded it to the ground. Why is this last one hanging on? What made its stem so minutely stronger?

> *JF looks again; turns back to the audience again.*

And in the second it takes us to marvel at its tenacity, there is a wind come up. The leaf flutters and protests. It leans back against a branch. As if resting. A new breeze flings it forward again. I can see that stubborn stem tear. The leaf unites with the open air.

(The poem:) "This is the time!"
This is the time!
This is the time!

    JF leaves.

    The End

Into

for Margaret Carley

Production Information

Into is inspired by the Julio Cortazar short story "The Southern Thruway".

Into exists in two versions. The original, shorter version—about 60 minutes—was first produced at the Toronto Fringe Festival in 1993, and is available in a Playwrights Canada Press edition with *Taking Liberties.* This version is about 85 minutes in length and was first produced at Theatre Passe Muraille in Toronto, in a co-production between that theatre and Theatre Cognito. The production ran from September 27 to October 30, 1994. The cast and production team was as follows:

BUSINESSMAN: Geoffrey Bowes
URBAN NUN: Marium Carvell
BOY: Michael Waller
LUCY: Gina Wilkinson

Director: Bill Lane
Assistant Director: Jocelyn Hublau
Designer: Glenn Davidson
Sound Design: Jack Nicholsen and Paul Tedeschini
Stage Manager: Janet Gregor
Assistant Stage Manager: Bella Srubiski
Technical: Nathaniel Kennedy and Bill Anderson

The time is slightly in the future. The setting is a freeway, one hour east of the metropolis.

Into

NUN is alone on stage.

NUN: I'm an urban nun.

I take my God with smoke.

I like him loud;

Rumbling like the Queen car,

Howling drunk,

Crazy with despair,

A thorn in the side,

A kick in the gut.

Don't want him leafy:

Gold leafy, green leafy, palm leafy.

Don't want him pastoral;

Pastoral is death.

And yeah, yeah, death's a comfort

But comfort is false.

A letter appears magically.

So this comes:

An invitation.

To an up-north, get-down Nunfest.

A Retreat for all the remaindered nuns of the world.

The valiant last two hundred.

All of us called

To a fine and quiet place

Of birds and bugs.

And birds.

And bugs.

And bugs.

And bugs.

So many, many bugs.

    Long, disgusted sigh.

Nuns alfresco.

(Reading.) "In God's own perfect nature."

I think not.

If nature's so perfect, God won't be there.

What's for him to do?

Relax?

God's going to relax?

Maybe he's going to lie under a tree

And daydream new plagues?

Right.

    Remembers letter. Shrugs.

But I go.

If only to remember what my sisters look like.

Hey—even nuns get nostalgic!

We get lonely!

I get lonely!

I'll often dig out my convent yearbook

On a slow Saturday night

And imagine proms that never were,

Football games never cheered,

Clash Days that faded into black and white.

I'll recall novices who slipped

On the trip up God's altar.

And I'll curse the sisters who never visit me

Because of the trough of incorrectness

In which I wallow.

    Sound under grows. Magical. Nature.

We retreat by bus and car,

Minivan, multivan, mountain bike.

Some hobble up the northern concessions—

Barefoot Nuns of Perpetual Atonement—

Grateful for the gravel,

The sharper the better.

And arriving by floatplane?

You guessed it—the Yankee Techno Nuns.

We're met by Sister Katherine.

Kate the Innocent.

My convent bunkmate way back when.

A vestal goofball sap

With a Saran Wrap smile.

Kate welcomes us to the lodge,

Her arms upraised

Like a Rio statue.

> *For just a second NUN raises her arms. Traffic has*
> *been building under her.*

Naturally, there's an orientation cocktail party.

And yes, the jokes are just what you'd expect

From a giggle of Godbrides:

Requests for Virgin Marys.

Purple Jesuses.

Rusty Nails.

But funny thing: the walls of isolation

Begin tumbling like Jericho.

We're so diverse, this last two hundred.

We're so international.

We're so intercultural.

Yet we're also interlinked

By this umbilical wince of faith.

A tender bond, fortified with booze.

So: when Sister Kate gets out her singing nun
guitar?

And warbles "Kumbaya"?

Like a Kate Bush with hymen?

Well, shut up!

Show some respect!

A musical cliché chased with Scotch

Can cure any sister's blues.

And: when Sister Kate suggests a little splish-splash?

Don't even think about laughing!

God's tilted the world into darkness.

His moon is warming the lake.

His sand fleas are urging us off the beach.

So we strip!

And we run!

No shit!

Carmelites, Ursulines, Josephines, Magdalenes!

Militants, Pacifists, Militant-Pacifists!

New Agers, Mainliners, Hardliners, One Liners!

Sounds of rising joy, splashing, happiness.

The chaste—and the chased!

The dogmatic, the pragmatic, the stigmatic!

The night is filled with the rustle of shedding habits!

Falling wimples muffling fleabeach!

Twittering like a hundred plucked ravens

We pound over naked sand!

An army of motoring legs and arms!

We immerse in the northern waters!

Two hundred throats—gasp!

Four hundred nipples—pop!

It's a glory of dunking sisters!

It's a nubile of nuntits!

Nuntits! Nunarms! Nunbushes!

Dark, sacred nunbushes!

Oh baby baby!

I float out on my back, past them all.

I look up at the moon and the stars—

Stars that might spell "God"

(If anyone could remember the language)

And I say, "Things don't get much better than this."

Exactly.

They start getting worse.

A lesbian nun-caucus has formed on the raft.

How do I know it's a lesbian nun-caucus?

They're debating the theology of Anne Murray.

"Who exactly is Snowbird?"

I swim in and think about getting up, but they glare.

They don't extend the helping hand.

They know I'm a straight celibate.

I ask, "Guys, guys! If you're not doing it—then

what does it matter who you're not doing it with?"

But the raft is oppressed and unfriendly.

The raft talks in code.

Some stars twinkle out.

On shore, squabbling is erupting over beached habits!

We've existed in such isolation

It never occurred to us to sew on labels.

And, in the dark,

The traditional black,

The healing white,

The post-modern blue,

Even the floatplane chinos of the Yankee Technos—

It all looks the same!

Some sound up, under, maybe buzzing.

We stand and argue,

And the local mosquitoes gorge

On our precious blood.

More stars fall.

God sees the little bastards fall.

And it's not the kind of falling that excited wishes.

Is it.

Moment of pause.

Next day, Kate the Innocent announces activities.

Morning is for: "Silence, light crafts, non-competitive prayer."

Afternoon, however, is a feast of options:

Seminars run by every faction;

Exercises in self-affirmation—

If it's your faction,

Exclusion if it's not.

The Yankees go up in the plane.

They're videotaping God.

Close-up.

The universe has 500 channels now.

One of them will buy God on shaky cam.

The advocates of a female God

Huddle over their Bibles

Frantically changing pronouns.

A cheer goes up as each He falls to a She.

The Atoners are rolling about a bed of poison ivy,

Pissing themselves with joy.

They swell.

They itch.

Nearer to their God they scratch.

I'm an urban nun but there's no urban option,

So I go all the way:

I take the St. Francis.

Bird-watching.

But even here there's dissent.

There are those who will only count vegetarian birds.

Not raptors. Not ones with claws.

Some note the superior plumage of the males

And, out of jealousy, count only the females.

Which brings them a kind of joy, because

"Blessed are the envious for they probably have less."

Less being more holy.

Envy therefore being more righteous.

Such is the logic of nuns with binoculars.

A magic gong.

Ah! That'll be the dinner bell.

The Cardinal's coming.

Cardinal A.

You know who I'm talking about.

The Big Silk.

The Grand Old Fart!

That silken redundant whiff of ecclesiastical flatulence.

But I digress.

No one's going in the dining hall!

There's controversy on the lawn!

The Macro-Feminists are organizing a boycott.

They're saying a male Cardinal shouldn't address
a Retreat of female Sisters.

All this time the Cardinal's limo is idling.

His Eminence is waiting for a friendly nod.

Kate the Innocent thinks fast!

"His penis has been inactive since World War II!

Where lies the problem!"

A leading Macro glares back.

"The problem, sister, lies not with the dormant
dangler.

The problem stems from what that mini-flesh is
connected to:

One hundred and ninety pounds of suppressed
testosterone."

A compromise is proposed.

By the Canadian nuns.

The Cardinal is declared an Honorary Woman.

But his virile driver is locked in the limo

Where he ogles and plots.

(More on the driver later.)

Under—a start to the traffic.

I've never actually seen Our Cardinal.

Our Cardinal lives in Rosedale.

In a great big mansion.

On a tiny perfect street.

I work in Parkdale.

On a road with aching shoulders.

I work.

I WORK!

Struggling to stay under control.

Our paths of righteousness never cross.

The Cardinal lectures us on Obedience.

He wants us to obey.

"Girls: obey."

Well excuse me, Mr. Cardinal:

What do you know that's worth obeying!

How dare you tell me to obey!

I don't even have time to OBEY!

Someone—I don't know who—throws a bun.

OK OK, I do know who.

T'was I.

All star pitcher, Triple A Convent League.

I rise to my feet.

Bun appears magically.

I grip the bun in my hand.

It burns my palm like hot salt.

I wind up.

OBEY THIS, YOU PIG!

NUN throws—perfect form. Oomph sound from Off.

Nailed him!

Square in the pre-War nuts!

He's going serious grey.

The hall's going dead silent.

Until:

> *Sound of applause, wild track "Urban Nun"*
> *chanting.*

Thank you thank you! Thank you very much!

My first standing O! Oh, this is quite nice.

I could enjoy this. Thank you. Thank you.

And now! A cathartic rain of pumpernickel!

And—snowballs made of hashbrowns!

Honeypots! Jampots!

And, from an ancient Carmelite who vaguely
remembers a 1965 Tom Jones concert:

Her immaculate panties!

The Cardinal "obeys" the laws of bun-bardment.

He falls!

The Cardinal "obeys" the laws of gravity.

He hits the dining hall floor!

Hard!

> *Dead silence.*

But his death?

Oh, that was from natural causes, no question.

We all agreed on that.

His—virile—driver dragged him off while we watched in silence.

We're so diverse this last two hundred.

And our collective awe stills our voices.

But remember? I don't like silence.

I'm an urban nun.

Silence is pastoral.

So I throw another bun.

At the Atoners.

Easy targets—they're puffed up like zeppelins.

When they glare back

With hate in their itchy-pig eyes,

I blame the Carmelites, and duck.

A minute later the dining hall's filled with missiles.

Everyone's beaning everyone who does not share their exact monopoly on grievance.

Good! I say.

To hell with this fiction of Nuns in Paradise.

We're too intercultural!

We're too transglobal!

There are 500 channels

And we're all surfing different waves.

I run out of there.

I howl at the moon until it begins to shake.

God's shivering behind it.

He knows how far I can hurl my anger.

He sees that babel of bunning nuns.

He knows he could be next.

    NUN is now almost completely in the moment.

I've got to get out of here!

I've got to get back to the city!

I leave a note for my friend Kate.

Come to my neck of the woods!

Come weep for my people!

And I drive off.

I drive past the dead Cardinal's limo.

The Cardinal's in the trunk now.

His driver's taking his time leaving.

His driver is a man with a plan.

His driver is an auto-alchemist.

The virile worm is changing into silk.

    Sound of traffic.

I have left my sisters behind.

They are not of my kind.

And now: I'm just another human

Hurtling along this vast, trackless highway.

Aw hell!

Brake lights!

Flashing now.

Flashing!

Flashing into the horizon.

Magic start to the jam. The other three characters now appear.

BUSINESSMAN: Damn!

LUCY: *(Into her Dictaphone tape recorder.)* Shit!

BOY: Fuck not again!

NUN: I'm just a nun, in a jam.

They all look at each other, though they are careful not to get caught. BOY may toss a wrapper out of his car, the first of many, and pop open a beer, also the first of many. LUCY stretches and speaks into her Dictaphone.

LUCY: Addendum 7B. Flight from Montreal. Stuck in traffic with: a youth. White. Surly. And some kind of Nun. *(Seeing BUSINESSMAN.)* And could it be? Could I be this lucky!?

LUCY looks away quickly, as BUSINESSMAN gets out of his car and wanders with his cell phone. LUCY watches surreptitiously.

BUSINESSMAN: I left the boathouse light on. The inside one. Can you get it? Yes, that's all I'm calling about, what else would I be calling for. I want you to turn the light off so the goddamn boathouse doesn't get full of bugs and they don't all stick to the goddamn canoe you made me varnish on my two days off. Please. No, I'm not in Toronto, I'm stuck in traffic. You phoned the house. Why'd you phone (the house?) *(Fear.)* Are the kids OK? *(Anger.)* Then why'd you phone home! *(Beginning to notice LUCY, who is stuck beside him.)* Even if I wasn't stuck here I wouldn't be there yet. Jesus Christ Claire!

BUSINESSMAN clicks off cell with a vengeance.
NUN is circling about. LUCY speaks into her tape
recorder, capturing key overheard phrases. Soon she
will get out of her car, and attempt to get closer to
BUSINESSMAN. He punches in another number.

(Talking in his phone, but also with an eye on LUCY.)
Charlie, I've got it: We merge top end literature
and cola. I want you to think about it. Wait:
literature, cola and something primary. Something
out of the ground. I don't know. Chrome. What do
you mean, you don't mine chrome? What does
chrome do—grow on trees? OK, then think of
something else. But we've got to look good
tomorrow, Chuckie. We've got to raise some
eyebrows, and merging macaroni and tomato
paste ain't gonna do it. Listen, I'm stuck in traffic;
I'll call you as soon as I get in—I've got another—
meeting, but I'll call you first.

BUSINESSMAN hangs up. NUN is out of her car,
stretching and strolling a bit. She's looked into
BUSINESSMAN's car. She starts to sing a snippet
of "Kumbaya", and then slaps herself.

NUN: Sister, get a life!

BOY litters with astounding and magical finesse.
LUCY, NUN and BUSINESSMAN all watch him;
BOY glares back. BUSINESSMAN dials phone
again.

BUSINESSMAN: Sorry. Claire, I'm sorry. I shouldn't have hung
up—on you.

This time BUSINESSMAN has been hung up on.
He shakes receiver.

Fuck you!

BOY opens another beer can. BUSINESSMAN,
BOY and LUCY have all turned their cars off.

You may as well turn your car off.

NUN: Sorry—were you talking to me?

BUSINESSMAN: We're not going anywhere.

NUN: It's an outrage!

BUSINESSMAN: Happens every weekend.

NUN: I never travel. It's new to me. When I rented my car they didn't warn me about traffic jams.

LUCY has overheard the last, and laughs, then whispers into her recorder. NUN glares. BOY drinks loudly. BUSINESSMAN taps in a new number.

BUSINESSMAN: OK Charlie: really high-end literature, as high as it gets. And really good cola. But skip the mining thing—we'll merge with a third world country. One of those itty bitty ones. New Zealand. Wait: nix the cola. Try Kleenex. High-end Kleenex. Thick stuff with Laura Ashley patterns. The kind my wife blows her nose in.

Time passes. BUSINESSMAN has wandered to the side of the highway.

NUN: *(To herself, aloud.)* How long will this last? Oh I say, how long, Lord, will this last. *(Getting into it a bit.)* Oh Lord, how long *(Etc.)*

LUCY: We could be here an hour.

NUN: Huh? An hour? What causes it—an accident?

LUCY: Could be as simple as too many cars.

NUN: It makes no sense.

LUCY: There's no logic to the behaviour of jams. They form and, when they break up, there's no logic to that, either.

Time passes. BOY explodes in another burst of litter and tears his Walkman off. BUSINESSMAN has returned.

BOY: No way!

BUSINESSMAN: What'd he say?

BOY: No way!

NUN: No way.

BOY: No way! The Rouge has flooded!

BUSINESSMAN: What about the Rouge?

NUN: He says it's flooding. Is that possible?

BUSINESSMAN: That's ridiculous. It's not even a river anymore. There's been no rain for a month. How does he think a flood happens without rain. Christ! This is our school system.

BOY gives BUSINESSMAN the finger. Time passes.

LUCY: I just heard on my radio that our Prime Minister and the President of Sudan are meeting at the airport. There's a motorcade, and that's what's causing this.

NUN: Makes more sense than a flood.

BUSINESSMAN: What'd she say?

NUN: There's a motorcade in the city.

BUSINESSMAN: That's absurd.

LUCY: Did he say "absurd"? It was on my radio. I heard it clearly. He said absurd? *(Into recorder.)* The absurd just called the absurd absurd. Absurd.

Time passes.

BUSINESSMAN: *(Tapping into his phone.)* Charlie—I'm still in traffic. I don't know what the hell's going on, but it's been an hour and we haven't budged. *(Moving off.)* Start the proposal without me.

> *Time passes. LUCY is snooping around BUSINESSMAN's car. The NUN catches her..*

LUCY: *(Guiltily, changing subject.)* I don't mean to pry, but are you a

NUN: —Yes yes, I'm a nun.

LUCY: I thought so. Which order?

NUN: Random.

> *No response.*

Sorry. Nun-joke.

LUCY: Oh I got it. I've heard it before, that's all. I was a Catholic. There were nuns in my school. They were always cracking jokes. What makes nuns so funny?

NUN: The absence of men.

LUCY: Then I should be a barrel of laughs.

NUN: *(Laughs.)* Any word on that "absurd" motorcade?

LUCY: Apparently the President of Sudan doesn't actually have the time or the inclination to go into the city, so they're driving about the top of Toronto. Back and forth. It's a particularly huge motorcade, to honour the President's status.

> *BUSINESSMAN has returned, and is trying to listen.*

NUN: You know why he's here, of course.

LUCY: Is that one of those existential questions? I'm really lousy at them.

NUN: Why he's in the country. The President of Sudan.
                (So BUSINESSMAN can hear.) He's a war criminal.

BUSINESSMAN: Are you talking to me?

NUN: They're committing a holocaust in Sudan and
                we're supplying them with everything they need.
                No one writes about it because the links between
                the arms suppliers and our media run too deep.

BUSINESSMAN: I know all this. The Sudanese are obsessed with
                weaponry and we're obsessed with selling it.
                Amazing how easily our cultures intersect.

NUN: Well, I think it's criminal.

BUSINESSMAN: And so it is. It should be stopped.

LUCY: He wants it to end?

NUN: I'm trying to stop it.

BUSINESSMAN: I have no doubt you are. But it'll take more than
                grade school finger-pointing.

NUN: I'm sorry. Your back seat is full of briefcases. So
                naturally I thought you'd endorse repression.

                *BOY throws a beer can out his window. The others
                all watch and register.*

LUCY: *(With Dictaphone.)* What exactly is in your
                briefcases?

BUSINESSMAN: Kleenex. Cola. Literature.

LUCY: *(Into Dictaphone.)* Cola, literature. *(Not believing.)*
                May I see?

BUSINESSMAN: No.

NUN: I should know better than to judge on externals. It
                just shows how conditioned we are to think
                businessmen are immoral.

BUSINESSMAN: We are immoral.

LUCY: Ah—a confession! *(To NUN.)* You must like that.

BUSINESSMAN: But you're immoral too. The difference is I provide jobs.

NUN: This is all somewhat arguable. Yet you know about Sudan.

BUSINESSMAN: We talk of nothing else. I'm a businessman who merges companies and products and countries and, let me tell you, it's a very peaceful trade. You can't merge amid chaos.

> *LUCY gets out of her car and stretches. BUSINESSMAN is clearly distracted. He has picked up his phone and is about to make a call.*

NUN: Why do you merge? I thought Big was out.

BUSINESSMAN: *(Into phone, distracted, watching LUCY.)* In some areas.

NUN: Take IBM. Its bigness made it vulnerable.

BUSINESSMAN: That had nothing to do with size. *(Puts phone away discreetly.)* It was a button-down patriarchy. That's death now. But you know something—I could say the same about the church.

NUN: You belong?

BUSINESSMAN: Of course not. But I know the Cardinal.

NUN: You know Cardinal A.

BUSINESSMAN: —Cardinal A. The Big Silk. He lives on my street. My wife and I are having him over for a barbeque next week. The kids love him. It's the robes—they think he's Mr. Dress-up.

LUCY: *(Returning.)* Has anyone heard anything?

NUN: —The Cardinal's a reactionary pig.

BUSINESSMAN: Perhaps if you sat down with him over a hamburger you'd feel differently.

LUCY: I was very close to our parish priest in Montreal. He wasn't much for burgers though. Pasta yes. But he was locked in a spiral of despair, and working for the church requires optimism.

NUN: That it does.

> *Time passes. BOY wanders off. BUSINESSMAN is back on his phone.*

Is this damn thing ever going to break up?

> *LUCY shrugs.*

Why do people travel?

LUCY: Beats me.

NUN: Why are you?

LUCY: What I'm doing isn't travel. It's flight.

NUN: Oh. Do you want to talk about it?

LUCY: Not really.

> *BOY bursts back. He has a news-flash.*

BOY: Someone up ahead said a plane landed on the highway!

BUSINESSMAN: Makes more sense than the river flooding. Marginally.

BOY: It happens all the time. *(Aside.)* Asshole.

NUN: Perhaps the plane landed on the Sudanese motorcade and they all skidded into the Rouge. There was massive water displacement and

LUCY: *(Pulling off her headphones, with a laugh.)* —It says, on the pop station—that the local nuclear plant's melting down.

BUSINESSMAN: The classical band doesn't agree. A few minutes ago—just before we found out about the plane squishing the Prime Minister

BOY: —I never said that!

BUSINESSMAN: —The classical band announced a shortage of mushrooms.

BOY: Oh fuck, that's bad.

BUSINESSMAN: Edible ones! And now the streets of Toronto are choked with packs of anxious BMWs. Herds of distressed Audi. Desperately seeking shitake.

NUN: So many disasters. Should I check the religious channel?

LUCY: It'll say locusts.

BUSINESSMAN: Or confirm the flooding.

NUN: Or announce the Rapture.

            NUN, LUCY and BUSINESSMAN all laugh. BOY is clearly odd man out.

BOY: If we had a TV we'd know for sure.

NUN: What does it matter? We've become stuck. We'll become unstuck.

BUSINESSMAN: Ah—a fatalist.

NUN: Optimist.

LUCY: Depends what you're heading back to. *(To BUSINESSMAN.)* Wouldn't you agree?

            Suddenly there's the sound of engines starting, rising.

            What's that?

BOY: Start your engines!

> *Everyone rushes to their cars. There is a roar of engines starting; hopeful looks, then absolute quiet.*

BUSINESSMAN: Damn!

LUCY: Shit!

BOY: Fuck!

NUN: It's God's will.

> *NUN rolls her eyes—it's not what she believes at all. LUCY puts her Walkman back on. BUSINESSMAN gets his phone out. BOY wanders off again, perhaps littering. Time passes.*

BUSINESSMAN: *(On phone.)* Hi Jackie. I'm in a jam. About an hour out, but nothing's happening. Listen: Claire's suspicious. She's hovering, that's how I know. I can't go to the can without her hovering outside the door. I just called her—she doesn't even believe I'm stuck in traffic. She's been calling the house. Oh—the line's breaking up—sorry, I can't hear you. Why don't you go over to the house. I'll be there soon. *(Hangs up.)*

> *NUN is out of her car. She's flapping out her clothes.*

NUN: Everything's full of goddamn earwigs. I never could see this rural paradise thing.

BUSINESSMAN: Me neither. It's hell. You get out there, you're trapped. You can't exit. Your every move is watched. All you can do—is varnish.

LUCY: *(To NUN.)* Why's everything so damp?

NUN: I don't know.

BUSINESSMAN: We haven't had rain in weeks.

NUN: I just assumed dampness was integral to the backwoods experience. Ironically, the only thing that isn't damp is my bathing suit. I never used it.

LUCY: You don't swim?

NUN: Oh, I swim all right. I just didn't use the suit.

LUCY: Ah.

NUN: I paddled about as God made me.

LUCY: If you don't mind my asking—was it a romantic thing?

BUSINESSMAN: She's an Urban Nun for Christ's sake!

LUCY: She doesn't have to answer.

NUN: There was a man there, yes.

LUCY: See.

NUN: But he died.

LUCY: That's awful!

NUN: He was a reactionary pig.

BUSINESSMAN: Another one?

LUCY: *(With Dictaphone.)* How'd he die?

NUN: Bread.

And then, the sound of motors starting up again.

(Running to car.) OK—here we go!

BUSINESSMAN: Finally!

BOY has also returned to his car. Nothing happens; motor sounds die and everyone is exasperated.

Damn!

LUCY: Shit!

BOY: Fuck!

NUN: Why do you think that happens?

LUCY: Someone gets optimistic and passes it down the
                line.

BUSINESSMAN: In my business we call it a bull market.

NUN: In mine it's a second coming.

                Time passes.

LUCY: It's so hot.

BUSINESSMAN: They should build showers along here.

LUCY: Another hour and it'll cool off.

NUN: Another hour!

BUSINESSMAN: I have to be in the city by then!

LUCY: Why the rush? *(Laughs.)*

                *Motors start again in the distance, and then the four
                start their own engines. But there is no movement
                and the engines are cut quickly. There is less
                reaction.*

                I'm not falling for it next time.

NUN: You will.

LUCY: No I won't. I'll just stay out here and let everyone
                else make fools of themselves.

NUN: You have no capacity for faith.

LUCY: Faith doesn't move cars.

                *Burst of revolting music from BOY's car. The other
                three stare at him.*

BUSINESSMAN: Turn that down!

                No response.

                Turn it down!

NUN, LUCY &
BUSINESSMAN: TURN IT DOWN!

> *BUSINESSMAN goes over to BOY's car and hands him headphones.*

BUSINESSMAN: As long as we're stuck, use these, okay?

> *BOY glares.*

NUN: *(Sweetly.)* I'd appreciate it, my son.

LUCY: *(To BOY.)* Thank you.

> *BOY grudgingly takes earphones. BUSINESS-MAN returns to the others.*

NUN: Do your children play that stuff?

LUCY: They'd hardly be old enough yet.

BUSINESSMAN: How'd you know I had kids?

NUN: Your briefcases are interrupted by booster seats.

BUSINESSMAN: They're too young for his—stuff. But Claire takes them to violin. A house-full of Suzuki-ites. Can you imagine what that's like?

LUCY: Especially after a hard day's merging.

> *Time passes. NUN sleeps a bit. BUSINESSMAN returns to his car, gets his phone, paces about. He is aware of LUCY. She is eavesdropping, though pretending to be listening to her Walkman. She also makes notes into her Dictaphone, and will repeat sotto voce key phrases from BUSINESSMAN's conversation—e.g. "going nuts", "Jackie" and "Out of my control". BUSINESSMAN calls Jackie.*

BUSINESSMAN: *(On cell.)* We haven't moved in three hours! I'm going nuts. It's beginning to look like we'll be here right into the night. You still haven't heard? There are all sorts of rumours out here—plane crashes,

meltdowns. I know, it was going to be our night to
talk. Jackie: don't be like that. Please? This is out of
my control. And I don't know what to do. I can't
leave them; I can't stay. Are the kids better off with
me and Claire together and hardly speaking—or
with us apart, and fighting over custody? Shit, the
line's breaking up again.

> *BUSINESSMAN has ended up near LUCY's car.
> She notices him and takes her Walkman earphones
> off.*

LUCY: More mergers?

BUSINESSMAN: At this time of night?

LUCY: I doubt multinationals sit around waiting for
                 Monday morning. Your wife, then?

BUSINESSMAN: No.

LUCY: Squash partner.

BUSINESSMAN: I don't play.

LUCY: Your mistress.

BUSINESSMAN: I have three young children.

LUCY: Is that a denial or a rationalization?

BUSINESSMAN: They're at the cottage—a hundred miles that way.
                 And I've just spent two days with them.

LUCY: So you've earned a mistress.

BUSINESSMAN: *(A laugh.)* Are you a private eye?

LUCY: Just independently nosy. I grew up on a little cul-
                 de-sac in Montreal, where we knew everyone's
                 business. Now I live in Toronto, in a high-rise. No
                 one knows anything about anybody. I'm in gossip
                 withdrawal. A traffic jam's a godsend. What's her
                 exact age?

BUSINESSMAN: Thirty.

LUCY: Hmm.

BUSINESSMAN: What. Is that too old for a mistress?

LUCY: Depends. How old are you?

BUSINESSMAN: Ancient. 32. 34. 36. 37.

LUCY: It's OK for men to be old.

                BOY pops open a beer. Burps loudly, etc.

BOY: Parr-teee!

                NUN awakens with a start.

LUCY: Actually, the older men are, the better.

BUSINESSMAN: Would you like one?

LUCY: I'd love one. I'm dying of thirst.

NUN: Good luck.

                *BUSINESSMAN goes to BOY, who is oblivious to
                his approach—his earphones are on and his music is
                full blast.*

BUSINESSMAN: Could I buy a couple?

                No answer.

                Excuse me!

                No answer.

                HEY!

                *BUSINESSMAN touches BOY, who jumps out of
                his skin.*

BOY: DON'T SHOOT!

BUSINESSMAN: Can I buy a couple of beers?

BOY: Fuck man—don't creep up on me like that!

BUSINESSMAN: It was kind of hard not to. Will you sell me some
                beer?

BOY: How long d'you think we'll be here?

BUSINESSMAN: Another hour?

BOY: I don't wanna run out. I ran out last Sunday. It's no
                fucking way to spend the night.

BUSINESSMAN: Could two make a difference?

BOY: It might.

BUSINESSMAN: Ten bucks?

BOY: Each?

BUSINESSMAN: Sure.

BOY: Cool.

                *BOY gives BUSINESSMAN two beers.
                BUSINESSMAN returns to LUCY. He opens the
                cans and hands one to her. He is expecting a
                conversation to ensue.*

LUCY: Thank you.

                *LUCY drinks long and cools her forehead with her
                can. BUSINESSMAN still expects a conversation,
                but LUCY ignores him. She rolls the can around her
                body, cooling herself, enjoying his attention and,
                just when he appears to be giving up, she pours a
                stream of beer down her front.*

BUSINESSMAN: My kingdom for a shower.

LUCY: Is that what you do with them?

BUSINESSMAN: Who's them.

LUCY: Them with whom you merge.

NUN: Why would he shower with a bunch of businessmen?

LUCY: Come on—do you shower with them?

NUN: Even priests don't shower in groups.

LUCY: Do you?

NUN: At least not anymore.

BUSINESSMAN: Yes.

NUN: Yes!

LUCY: How many mistresses can fit under a showerhead?

NUN: That is an incredibly weird question.

LUCY: I wasn't asking you.

> *NUN moves off a bit. BUSINESSMAN comes close to LUCY.*

BUSINESSMAN: Look, I can ask you things too. What about you? What do you do with men?

LUCY: Hunt them.

BUSINESSMAN: Oh. *(Moving off.)* I would ask.

> *Time passes.*

NUN: An entire night. Such are the dangers of leaving the downtown core.

> *Time passes. BOY tosses out a crumpled beer can.*

BOY: I knew I'd run out.

> *Time passes.*

BUSINESSMAN: *(On cell.)* Yes I'm still in the jam goddamn it! *(Slams phone down.)* She doesn't believe me.

> *Time passes.*

LUCY: A shower! Thirty-six hours without a shower!

              Time passes.

NUN: Three days without a cigarette!

BOY: It makes me really mad.

NUN: At night I dream of the good old days when you could sit in a café, any café, and in minutes an illicit man would smuggle up to you with a pulsating gym bag and whisper promises of cut-rate DuMaurier. Oh, where is such a man to be found? Be still, urban lungs, be still.

BOY: That's Shakespeare, right?

NUN: Uh, yes.

BOY: I knew it.

NUN: Come with me.

BOY: Why?

NUN: Some of our neighbours make me nervous and I need a guard.

BOY: What for?

NUN: An urgency must be satisfied behind yonder bush.

              NUN and BOY are exiting.

BOY: That's Shakespeare too. I flunked it but I definitely remember the word "yonder". And there was a bush, now that I think of it.

NUN: Actually, it was a forest.

BOY: Yeah, and the forest moved. Weird. Aliens, probably. Shakespeare really makes me mad.

              Time passes. Light back up on BUSINESSMAN and LUCY. They are sharing a drink. They toast.

> *NUN returns at some point, but stays in her car.*

BUSINESSMAN: Happy hunting.

LUCY: Joyful merging.

BUSINESSMAN: So you've had three days—what kind of game have you bagged so far?

LUCY: What do you mean?

BUSINESSMAN: You say you hunt men, but I haven't seen you dragging any home to your car yet.

LUCY: First of all, the pickings nearby aren't very good. Look at that bunch behind us—all they do is eat potato chips.

BUSINESSMAN: They are pretty disgusting. I asked them if they wanted to join our aerobics this morning—they just laughed at me.

LUCY: Anyway, I'm not hunting new game. I'm updating my data on the old.

BUSINESSMAN: What's that mean?

LUCY: You really haven't seen me before?

BUSINESSMAN: What—before the last three days? No.

LUCY: Never on your street?

BUSINESSMAN: No—why—do you live in Rosedale?

LUCY: Never in the lobby of your office building?

BUSINESSMAN: What is this—where's Nun.

LUCY: Off getting food. Don't change the subject. You've never seen me at—say—the Art Gallery?

BUSINESSMAN: Paintings bore me.

LUCY: What about sculpture? You like sculpture.

BUSINESSMAN picks up phone. Dials.

BUSINESSMAN: Hi Pumpkin. What're you doing, Pumpkin. Yeah, I can talk to mummy later; I just want to talk with you now. Yeah. So what've you been doing...

BUSINESSMAN walks off, rebuffing LUCY. Time passes, a day. Light comes up on BOY. He is looking down at the Cardinal's corpse in the trunk of His Eminence's limousine.

BOY: This is incredible. It's like on TV. Wait—don't close the trunk yet. Two more minutes, please. *(Gets close, reacts to smell.)* Wow. He's really— *(Reaches down and tastes something.)* Strawberry?

NUN: *(Off.)* Where are you?!

BOY: Fuck, I gotta go!

BOY exits. Light goes off him, back on jam. Time passes. BUSINESSMAN is on the phone.

BUSINESSMAN: Charlie! Where are you! What's this voice mail shit. Why aren't you picking up your messages? Get back to me. *(Hangs up.)*

LUCY: Trouble in merger-land?

BUSINESSMAN: It's my flunkie.

LUCY: Charlie Maxwell.

BUSINESSMAN: He's been avoiding me. He hasn't returned my calls in a week. How'd you know his name?

LUCY: I've got a file on him, too.

BUSINESSMAN: A file?

LUCY: Charlie gets around.

BUSINESSMAN: Charlie? Not sexually. Charlie? No way. He does? Where.

LUCY: Your golf club. Wednesday afternoons.

BUSINESSMAN: That's Ladies' Day!

LUCY: And Charlie's there, practising his stroke. Chipping and putting and huffing in the rough.

BUSINESSMAN: You really have a file on me?

LUCY: It's very thick.

BUSINESSMAN: It is?

LUCY: This is an auspicious coincidence.

BUSINESSMAN: How?

LUCY: There's a million cars out here and we're stuck together. I thought I saw you about fifty miles back, but for some reason I'd thought you cottaged north of the city, not east, so I dismissed it from my mind. Then traffic stopped and I realized my assumptions about your summer life were wrong and

BUSINESSMAN: —You really saw me at the Art Gallery?

LUCY: Many times.

BUSINESSMAN: I—I find the sculptures—in the Moore Gallery— comforting.

LUCY: Comfort is false. You're there because you'll connect with someone. I'm there to watch. I've searched all over the city for the right place—and finally I found it: the Moore. It's safe, there are guards, there are shadows, shapes you can step behind. And it's teeming with heterosexual men. I couldn't believe my luck when I stumbled on it— the last untapped reservoir of straight men— intelligent straight men—in the city. Throngs of them, every night, all of you stopping in on your way home for a thousand murky reasons.

BUSINESSMAN: Why me?

LUCY: Why not?

BUSINESSMAN: But if it was "teeming"

LUCY: —You were unusually active.

BUSINESSMAN: I was?

              LUCY nods.

              Oh God.

LUCY: I was grateful.

BUSINESSMAN: You were?

LUCY: My favourite files are on my Moore men. I have
              affairs with them—on paper. *(Pause.)* I was having
              a really hot one with you. According to my files,
              you're very, very good.

BUSINESSMAN: I am?

LUCY: Exceptionally.

BUSINESSMAN: No shit.

LUCY: So good, in fact, that last week something strange
              happened. I saw you connecting with all those
              women and I began wondering if maybe it couldn't
              happen to me, too. And not just on paper. So I went
              back to Montreal. Actually, I was going back for a
              funeral but that's the perfect time to rekindle an old
              love, isn't it. I'm very good at funerals. I cry well.
              Men find that attractive. And I was seized with
              optimism that one soured love, in particular, might
              uncurdle.

BUSINESSMAN: And did it?

LUCY: No. No chance. I made an absolute fool of myself.
              I'm susceptible to hope and that's always the

result. So it's back to the files. It's bet academic.

BUSINESSMAN: So—what's the status of our paper affair—are we still an item?

LUCY: Getting rocky.

BUSINESSMAN: Because of Claire?

LUCY: You promise to leave her—and then the weekend comes and you're driving up north—east—to be with her.

BUSINESSMAN: Trust me, it's not her, it's the kids.

LUCY: It's all the same to a mistress. My paper affairs always end after three or four months, when I get bored. The real challenge is to create that accurate biography. Because I prize accuracy. The stalking becomes very sophisticated. I have to know where you live—that's easy—what you eat—easy—and where. Easy. Who you usually sleep with—easy. Who you occasionally sleep with—fairly easy. You do leave a trail. But what you really think and feel—and fear? That's the challenge. Oh God, how much longer will this last?

BUSINESSMAN: *(Still stunned.)* I have no idea.

LUCY: Because I want a shower. I dream of showers. I've been dreaming of nothing but, for the last seven days.

> *Time passes. NUN and BOY return with food. NUN is harrying BOY along.*

BOY: Check this out! Look at the food she scored!

NUN: Careful!

BOY: She's fucking—sorry—amazing!

NUN: God is amazing. I simply threaten.

LUCY:	*(Helping BOY.)* Now see? We're not so bad, are we. I bet no one else has food this good.
NUN:	One week in a jam and you can scare anything out of anybody.
LUCY:	This is your best haul yet.
BUSINESSMAN:	*(To BOY.)* The meat goes in your cooler
BOY:	—I know I know
BUSINESSMAN:	—And the canned goods in her trunk and

LUCY holds up a bag of chips.

NUN:	—Even the Chip-eaters respond to threats from God's little surrogate.

Cheers. Bag is opened, all share.

LUCY:	Any news?
NUN:	The usual gothic rumours. One group says there are riots in the city and they don't dare let us back in.
BOY:	They're calling in the Marines.
BUSINESSMAN:	We don't have Marines.
BOY:	Yes we do.
BUSINESSMAN:	No we don't.
BOY:	Yes we do.
BUSINESSMAN:	Here in Canada, we don't have Marines.
BOY:	Where there is water there are Marines. And, in Canada—in case you haven't noticed—we have lots of water. Therefore we have lots of Marines.
BUSINESSMAN:	You—are—very—very—thick.

BUSINESSMAN and BOY glare at each other.

LUCY: Where's the rioting?

NUN: All through the suburbs.

LUCY: But who?

NUN: Disaffected white youths.

BUSINESSMAN: Who told you this?

NUN: Other disaffected white youths. There's a cluster of them a half mile down.

BUSINESSMAN: It was probably just a ploy to guilt food out of you.

BOY: Yeah, well I believed them. I know where they're coming from. People are really mad now. Me and my friends can't even go to the mall without somebody making us mad. It really makes me mad.

BUSINESSMAN: Mad at what?

BOY: If you don't know, then you don't understand.

BUSINESSMAN: *(Repeats; mystified.)* If I don't know I don't understand

BOY: —You don't know where I'm coming from.

BUSINESSMAN: Fine. I don't know. I'll have to wallow in ignorance. Poor me.

BOY: And it makes me really mad that nobody ever comes around and asks us why we're mad. Everyone else who's mad gets studied but not me and my buddies

BUSINESSMAN: *(To NUN, over BOY, of food.)* You did well.

BOY: —I'm still talking! You never let me finish anything. You think you know every fucking— sorry sister—thing. A. We have Marines. B. I'm white. C. I'm—what am I again.

NUN & LUCY: Disaffected.

BOY: So don't forget that. Treat me with dignity man.

BUSINESSMAN: Oh Jesus. OK. You're right. Sorry. Thank you very much for helping get all this food.

BOY: That's all I ask for. A little dignification.

NUN: It's going to get tougher. There are groups forming up and down the line and some of the units are big, really big. Four cars wide, ten deep. The Chip-eaters are benign in comparison. Some of the new groups have different ways of governing, and a few were reluctant to let us through, at least without paying a toll. Even when I told them I was a nun! Sometimes that made it worse! There's a depth to anti-nun sentiment I never dreamt possible.

BOY: There's a really cool group five down.

NUN: A terrifying coincidence has a convoy of youths together.

BOY: They've been partying all week!

NUN: The confederations around them are planning reprisals. You be glad you're here with us.

BOY: And there's a dead dude!

LUCY: What!

BOY: Yeah. He's stuffed in a trunk.

NUN: Where.

BOY: Thataway. In a limo.

NUN: A limo?

BUSINESSMAN: How'd you know he was dead?

BOY: He was wearing a sign. "Hi, I'm dead." Dough-head.

BUSINESSMAN: You are really getting on my nerves

LUCY: —Please?

BUSINESSMAN: Sorry.

NUN: What colour was the limousine?

BOY: Black.

NUN: Black.

BUSINESSMAN: How'd he die?

BOY: Oh, now you're all ears.

BUSINESSMAN: I said I was sorry.

BOY: I don't know how he died. But it looks like somebody kicked the shit out of him.

NUN: You actually saw him?

BOY: Yeah, this guy in a silk dress let me look.

BUSINESSMAN: There was a man in a silk dress.

BOY: It looked like something you'd wear to a prom.

NUN: (*Figuring it out, sotto.*) The driver

BOY: —I had to give the man in the dress some smokes. To let me look. It was worth every butt. The dead guy's got bruises all over his head. And he's covered in seeds.

BUSINESSMAN: Seeds!

BOY: And strawberry jam.

NUN: Raspberry.

BOY: It tasted like strawberry. I thought it was blood at first. Maybe the guy in the dress killed him. You never know. And all these people from the cars nearby are bringing the silk guy food and calling him, "Your Grace". That's so weird.

LUCY: What sort of man would wear a red silk dress—in a traffic jam?

BUSINESSMAN: Cardinal A!

NUN: NO! I mean, no. Don't be silly. Why would Cardinal A be out on a freeway with a dead man in his trunk?

BUSINESSMAN: I vaguely remember him saying he was going to address a—Retreat.

LUCY: Now there's a coincidence. Weren't you at a Retreat?

NUN: The Cardinal never leaves Rosedale. No, if it's a Cardinal back there, it's likely a Quebec one. Yeah. Or an Oshawa Cardinal. Yeah. The dead guy's probably his driver. They die all the time, those drivers. Stones hit them. From transports. He'll be decomposing. I'm decomposing. Is he—I mean, has he been wrapped up?

BOY: He's dead.

NUN: I've got to go there.

BUSINESSMAN: I'll come with you.

NUN: No!

BUSINESSMAN: You'll need a guard.

NUN: No!

BOY: Let's all go!

NUN: NO!

BUSINESSMAN: Why are you acting so strange?

NUN: It's a Catholic thing you wouldn't understand. OK.

	Where's my Bible? Figures I'd forget it. I'll have to wing it.
LUCY:	Wing what?
NUN:	The burial mass. Look. We don't need to dwell on this. You'll all end up getting depressed. I'll just go there and bury him.
LUCY:	Let me come.
NUN:	No.
LUCY:	I was Catholic.
NUN:	No.
LUCY:	I'm curious about death.
NUN:	No.
LUCY:	I can lend dignity to a service.
NUN:	No.
LUCY:	I know when to cry. I was just at a funeral in Montreal and I'm telling you, I really carried my weight in tears. *(Tears.)* Please, Sister, Please?
NUN:	Oh, all right. But no recording devices.
BUSINESSMAN:	We need some drink. Do you think your party pals have any alcohol?
BOY:	All gone. I asked. But they said there's a Molson's transport two miles behind us.
BUSINESSMAN:	That'll do. We'll buy some cases. For us.
BOY:	You better not be bullshitting me.
BUSINESSMAN:	We can do a purchase when they're off burying. Two miles?
BOY:	Man, I can't carry beer that far! I brought all the food back.

> *BOY goes to his car. LUCY and NUN are leaving.*

NUN: We won't be long.

BUSINESSMAN: Do you want to invite the Cardinal back?

NUN: Absolutely not.

BUSINESSMAN: But he'll be grieving for his driver.

NUN: The church has a glut of drivers. His grief will be fleeting.

> *LUCY is primping.*

Oh for God's sake Lucy—it's a funeral, not a dance.

LUCY: I've been to many funerals, but never one on an expressway. And never when I smelled this bad.

NUN: The corpse won't care. *(To BUSINESSMAN.)* And try to make amends. Please. He's a good kid.

LUCY: I think he's adorable!

BUSINESSMAN: You do? He's a menace!

NUN: We had a nice talk when we were out foraging. He's just trying to find himself.

BUSINESSMAN: There's nothing to find.

LUCY: He means well.

BUSINESSMAN: He's a simpleton.

NUN: No, he's a primitive. It's not the same thing. He's almost Rousseau-ian. Without the nature. Actually, he has absolutely no concept of nature.

BUSINESSMAN: His life's one big parking lot.

LUCY: He's a suburban savage.

NUN: I kind of like that.

LUCY and BUSINESSMAN look askance.

As a nun, for Pete's sake. Now come on, Luce. We've got some burying to do.

LUCY and NUN exit. BUSINESSMAN goes over to BOY.

BUSINESSMAN: I'll walk west and ask for water at one of the farmhouses. Then I'll go and buy us beer. Are you OK?

BOY doesn't answer.

Homesick?

BOY: Oh, as if you care.

BUSINESSMAN: Actually—I do—care. And I'm sorry if I've been doing—acting—treating you like—you know. You and me and Lucy and the Urban Nun—we've got to stick—hang—we've got to tough it out together and—well—you know—so, can we be friends?

BOY: Do we have Marines?

BUSINESSMAN: Wherever there's water.

BOY: And what do Marines do?

BUSINESSMAN: I believe they keep us free.

BOY: OK, we're friends.

BUSINESSMAN: That's good. Good. We're friends. It's good to be friends. Yup. Buddies. Buddies in a jam. So. So, pal. Uh—where are you from?

No response from BOY.

Pal, I'm trying to do a little bonding here, you know, you, me, guy-to-guy stuff. Help me, OK?

BOY: I'm from back thataway.

BUSINESSMAN: Oshawa?

BOY: Not exactly. It doesn't have a name. Over there, where 409 and 12 meet, just past that. I mean, behind the mall past that. Actually, the third mall. Three malls, four McDonalds, then you make a left at the eighth Gulf.

BUSINESSMAN: Ah. And where were you headed when this happened.

BOY: Thataway. To visit my brother. Other side of Toronto.

BUSINESSMAN: Mississauga?

BOY: Not exactly. It doesn't have a name. It's near where 400 crosses 800. You have to be taken there the first time by somebody who's already been, or you can't find it.

BUSINESSMAN: Then how did the first person get there?

BOY: Fuck, that's right! Somebody had to start things off. Evolution?

BUSINESSMAN: There's always the Big Bang theory. Did you study it? Of course not. Something collides—atoms or—or—

BOY: Neutrons

BUSINESSMAN: —or neutrons, and a whole suburb is born.

BOY: Or it could be aliens. They just dropped it down on a farm. Anything possible with those places. Where my brother lives, all the streets curve the same way and every house is exactly the same. Three times my brother's gone into the wrong house, sat in the wrong chair and started drinking somebody else's beer. He says if it was a different brand he'd have known it wasn't his place, but all three times it was the very same label. Weird.

BUSINESSMAN: It must be very tough on him living there.

BOY: It's not so bad. It's how he got his job. My brother was sitting in this rec room once eating pizza and drinking beer, and this stranger walks in the door. The stranger takes one look at my brother—and hires him! Turns out, it was actually the other guy's house. He was advertising a job, and he thought my brother was showing huge fucking balls to just walk in like that. And—get this: my brother was too smart to let on he'd missed his own rec room by four streets.

BUSINESSMAN: How old are you?

BOY: Nineteen. I'll be twenty in four months.

BUSINESSMAN: Where have you been?

BOY: Huh?

BUSINESSMAN: Have you ever travelled?

BOY: What d'ya call this?

BUSINESSMAN: Right. It's travelling. OK. *(Exiting.)* This has been a good chat. Talk. Rap. I'm going for the beer. I'll be back in an hour.

BOY: What'm I going to do?

BUSINESSMAN: Guard the cars. There could be looters. Or aliens.

                 BUSINESSMAN exits. Light up on NUN and LUCY. They are kneeling in front of what appears to be an open grave, looking down into it.

LUCY: He seems awfully old for a chauffeur.

NUN: The Church has a hard time finding drivers.

LUCY: But you said there was a glut!

NUN: —And it takes a unique man to drive a Cardinal.

	They're very bossy. And they won't travel on just any old road.
LUCY:	The Cardinal is so young. And virile. When I was a Catholic the Cardinals were all musty old coots who had no concept of reality.
NUN:	Yes, well, the church is struggling to renew itself. Many of our best Cardinals now are Generation X. OK, I'm going to start.
LUCY:	*(Reaching in and tasting.)* Why's he covered in pumpernickel seeds?
NUN:	It's the custom in certain dioceses. The seeds symbolize the life force. Are you going to ask questions all afternoon or can I begin.
LUCY:	Should I start crying now?
NUN:	Please.
LUCY:	Do you want heartfelt sobbing or a subdued weep? I can do both but the weep is more attractive.
NUN:	The weep will be fine.
LUCY:	I have this lovely Kleenex the Businessman gave me. I'll use it to effect.
NUN:	Fine.
LUCY:	He's merging Kleenex with New Zealand. Seems like an odd fit to me.
NUN:	Lucy! *(Starts.)* Bless me Father for I have sinned. It has been (a few weeks)—
LUCY:	—That's not the burial service!
NUN:	LUCY!
LUCY:	Well it's not! At a funeral certain proprieties must be observed. It's bad enough the Cardinal keeps grabbing my behind but now you're confessing—

NUN:	—SHUT UP AND WEEP!

LUCY begins weeping gently.

It has been a few weeks since my last confession but there have been mitigating circumstances. These, however, have been my sins: I have—I have—I have thrown objects.

LUCY is weeping well.

For that and all my sins I am heartily sorry. Oh Lucy, I've made a huge mistake, an epic one. I look at that poor sod all covered in seeds and I know that sure, sure, the pumpernickel didn't do much more than wound his dignity and, for sure it was the jam pots that finished him off—but I did throw that first bun.

LUCY: I'm really bad at this metaphysical stuff.

NUN: I killed that man.

LUCY: I suppose we all kill each other, in a way.

NUN: It felt good killing him.

LUCY: I don't understand this new liturgy.

NUN: Killing Cardinals is the logical expression of the powerlessness we feel.

LUCY: Oh, why can't we go back to the Latin?

NUN: But when morality collides with logic, shouldn't we keep our buns on the table.

LUCY: Latin is so much easier to not understand.

NUN: Yet as I kneel here and look at him, I still feel disgust, at him, at myself, at the church, at the world. At everyone but God. Maybe even at Him.

LUCY: Or Her.

NUN: Fuck off.

                Pause. LUCY is wounded.

                Aw Lucy, how do I make sense of it all? How can it
                all be balanced?

LUCY: Are you asking me?

NUN: Yes, dammit!

LUCY: I've never done Q and A at a funeral. Of course I've
                never been told to fuck off by a nun, either. Gosh.
                Balance. It's like how can I be with men when I
                don't want to be with them, but I do want to be
                with them. The question becomes: is it enough to
                keep accurate files?

NUN: I think we should go. I'll pray for him tonight. The
                Cardinal's got a nice bag of groceries for us and I'd
                like to get back to our cars before dark.

                NUN and LUCY are leaving.

LUCY: That wasn't as sad as I thought it would be. I think
                because we got on to that discussion thing.
                Ordinarily, I'm a faucet. Aren't you coming?

NUN: In a second.

                *LUCY is leaving. NUN looks down at the dead
                Cardinal once more.*

                Forgive me. *(Starts to leave, then turns back.)* Forgive
                me and I'll forgive you.

                *Light off LUCY and NUN. BUSINESSMAN
                returns to jam carrying beer. BOY is eating.*

BUSINESSMAN: *(Entering.)* Oh you're gong to be proud of me. The
                last case. It cost me but *(Sees BOY eating.)* What are
                you doing! What the fuck are you doing!

                BUSINESSMAN jumps BOY.

	What the hell are you doing!?
BOY:	What's it look like?
BUSINESSMAN:	That's our food!
BOY:	It's mine, too!
BUSINESSMAN:	Put that back! Spit it out!
BOY:	Go to hell!
BUSINESSMAN:	*(Pinning BOY.)* It's not your food! Get it? It's all of our food! It's everyone's! We divide it equally! We eat it together! Understand!
BOY:	Fuckhead Businessman.
BUSINESSMAN:	You know damn well everything we gather is shared equally! If I ever catch you doing this again, you're outa here, get it? You're off the freeway. Now get the hell in your car!
BOY:	No.
BUSINESSMAN:	I'll call the Marines!
BOY:	Oh, I'm scared. You didn't even know we had them until I told you. What's their phone number?
BUSINESSMAN:	You are indescribably stupid.
BOY:	Stop saying that! I'm smart! I'm just as smart as anyone! I'm sick of you treating me like that. I'm leaving! That's final! I'm outa here!
BUSINESSMAN:	And where will you go, my disaffected little friend?
BOY:	I'm joining the Chip-eaters.
BUSINESSMAN:	They won't have you. The Chip-eaters hate you. They hate your music, they're sick of your litter, they can't stand anyone who's thin. They don't want you. No one wants you. Oh—maybe the

disaffected white youths—you could try them.
You'd have a real blast with them. You could sit
around littering and complaining about the size of
your dicks.

BOY is gathering together his essential items.

BOY: You've wanted to get rid of me from the very
moment traffic stopped. OK, I'm going. Whose
case will you get on now, asshole?

*BOY leaves. BUSINESSMAN picks up his phone
and punches in a number.*

BUSINESSMAN: What do you mean it's disconnected? That's my
office!

BUSINESSMAN tries another number.

Hi Pumpkin. It's Daddy. Daddy. What do you
mean you'll "go get Daddy"—I'm Daddy! I'm your
Daddy, Pumpkin. I'm the Daddy Pumpkin,
Pumpkin. *(Pause.)* Who are you? Charlie? What're
you doing there? Charlie, what's going on! *(Pause.)*
He hung up on me!

*LUCY and NUN arrive back from funeral. LUCY is
busy theorizing, to NUN's annoyance.*

LUCY: The more I think of it, you may be on to something.
If you had confession at every funeral, the families
could unload all their guilt right at the gravesite.
And then, maybe you could add some happy
liturgy, like the Christmas service—you could
really send 'em home smiling. It would certainly
make people feel better about death. Though
maybe less good about Santa.

NUN: LUCY!

BUSINESSMAN: You've got more food!

NUN: The Cardinal's got every Catholic for miles
fetching him stuff.

BUSINESSMAN: How was the funeral?

LUCY: Avant garde.

NUN: Where's the Boy?

BUSINESSMAN: Gone.

LUCY: Gone!

BUSINESSMAN: I caught him stealing food.

NUN: He was stealing our food?

BUSINESSMAN: He doesn't understand the nature of co-ops. I don't know how to deal with him. Even my three year-old is more rational.

NUN: I'll talk to him when he gets back.

BUSINESSMAN: He's not coming back. He's off to join the Chip-eaters.

LUCY: But we need him here!

BUSINESSMAN: Why!? What's he adding to this?

LUCY: I don't know. Something.

BUSINESSMAN: He's useless!

NUN: He adds a bit of weight to our numbers.

LUCY: Yes!

NUN: We're the smallest group for miles.

LUCY: And he's someone for her to fuss over.

NUN: I don't fuss! But I do know that we'd better not get into the business of quantifying who has what value to this unit.

BUSINESSMAN: What's that supposed to mean?

NUN: It means that the only person actually getting food for us is me, because of my religious connections. Maybe I should go it alone. Maybe I should lock myself in my car and let you guys starve while I eat my Catholic face off.

LUCY: I thought we were friends!

NUN: I'm making a point. I'm going to wait a few hours for the Boy. If he's not back by tomorrow, we're going out searching for him. He's family and I want him home.

                 NUN goes off, leaving LUCY and BUSINESS-MAN. LUCY notices the phone in BUSINESS-MAN's hand and automatically reaches for her tape recorder.

LUCY: You were calling someone?

BUSINESSMAN: For the first time in three weeks.

LUCY: Five weeks, actually.

BUSINESSMAN: I can't remember most of the numbers now and—anyway, whenever I do make a call new people answer. It's really been five weeks?

LUCY: *(Consulting notepad.)* My last entry was a call you made to Charlie. You told his answering machine that he lacked corporate imagination. So who'd you phone?

BUSINESSMAN: My kids.

LUCY: Time of call.

BUSINESSMAN: Charlie was there.

LUCY: OK, but time of call. *(Throws down pen.)* Aw, what's the use. My records are already inaccurate. I'm not the academic I once was. I barely listen to the radio for news even. It's as if we've ceased to exist.

BUSINESSMAN: I have—for my kids.

Black on them, lights up on BOY. He is walking through an alien landscape, alone and terrified. He is confused as to directions, stumbles, maybe runs. But then he comes to the crest of the hill and is looking down on the Disaffected White Youths. He is filled with joy.

BOY: There they are! My people! Hey! HEY! Hey Hey!

Black on him. Light back on BUSINESSMAN and LUCY.

LUCY: Look at Nun. She's so upset about the Boy—she's praying he'll come back.

BUSINESSMAN: I over-reacted. I do the same thing with my kids. I hate when I do that. "It really makes me mad."

LUCY: I can't bear to think he's gone.

BUSINESSMAN: Funny. That boy epitomizes everything I hate about this country. He's ignorant. He's lazy. He can't think straight. And—I'm worried sick about him.

LUCY: It was one of the first things I put in your file.

BUSINESSMAN: What.

LUCY: Your conscience.

BUSINESSMAN: Really?

LUCY: Your capacity for feeling.

BUSINESSMAN: Is that what you were thinking—when you saw me at the Gallery?

LUCY: Oh, when I'm there, I'm not thinking.

BUSINESSMAN: Then what are you feeling?

LUCY: Desire.

BUSINESSMAN: What drives you to desire?

LUCY: Despair.

BUSINESSMAN: Despair to desire. And next?

LUCY: I kill the desire. Or maybe I sublimate it, to my research.

BUSINESSMAN: But wouldn't you rather live? Wouldn't you rather snatch a few months of really living?

LUCY: Those are lines. You're reverting.

BUSINESSMAN: They're not lines.

LUCY: They're in my files! I've heard you whispering them from the dark side of a dozen Henry Moores. They won't work with me. Try something else. Perhaps a sigh about, "The irony of being in mergers but remaining an isolated wanderer." That's the one you use on the literary types. Your Ulysses line. Or go one step further into danger. Try the truth.

BUSINESSMAN: OK. I wish I'd taken you home in March.

LUCY: Perhaps—oh—the weekend your wife and kids went skiing? You were already booked.

BUSINESSMAN: Then I wish I'd taken you home one afternoon.

LUCY: What—on a Wednesday, when poor Claire was off golfing and the children were napping with nanny? Not my style.

                Pause. NUN passes through.

NUN: No sign of him?

BUSINESSMAN: No.

NUN: I pray he had the sense to stay on the highway. He won't last a minute if he wanders into those trees.

                NUN continues to her car.

BUSINESSMAN: *(Leaving with LUCY.)* We'll finish this later.

LUCY: No doubt.

        Time passes. Light on NUN.

NUN: I want that Boy back. I want my Boy back. Send him back to me, God!

        BOY has appeared behind NUN, bruised and bloodied, his clothes torn.

BOY: Sister. Sister?

NUN: I swear I can

BOY: —Sister?

        BOY falls into NUN's arms. She eases him to the ground. Pieta time on the freeway.

NUN: What happened to you!? Here, let me get that.

        NUN props BOY up and begins cleaning his wounds.

BOY: I don't understand.

NUN: What.

BOY: I don't fucking sorry understand.

NUN: *(Calling off.)* LUCY! *(To BOY.)* What aren't you understanding?

LUCY: *(Running on, with BUSINESSMAN.)* Oh my God!

BOY: I don't understand why they hate me.

NUN: Who.

BUSINESSMAN: We don't hate you, son.

BOY: No, them. *(Indicates freeway.)* Back as far as you can see they hate me, they all hate me. I went looking for some other group to hang out with. Fine, I think, you guys don't want me? I'll go live with the Chip-eaters.

NUN: You'd trade us for them?

BOY: I said, "Hey there, Chip-eaters, what's happening?" And they yelled at me to screw off. And it was the same with the Dental Confederation. I said, "Hey Dentists, can I join you?" They told me to wait at the side of the road. They had these chairs set up and old magazines and a fish tank. That was cool, but I waited and I waited—until finally I realized it was a trick. A dentist trick. They were going to make me wait there till I rotted. Dentists make me mad. And after that it was just one thing after another. The Timid Zone set off their car alarms at the very sight of me. The Volvos promised they'd form a committee to see about letting me in. As if. Then there were the Anne Murrayites. They accused me of being a man. Thanks for the news-flash guys. And every other group turned me away until finally I got to the crest of the hill and there they were.

NUN: The Disaffected White Youth?

BOY: My people. As far as the eye could see. A whole valley-full. Their sweet music crashed up into my eardrums. I could smell hamburger cooking. Just like when you're sitting in your car at the back door of The Sizzle Pit waiting for your girlfriend to get off work. And there were babes. Real babes. Disaffected white babes. Not ones like up there with the Bourgeois Confederacy where they won't speak to you unless you're taking French fucking Immersion. These were real babes, with great big tattoos. I stood at the top of the hill and I say, "Hey! Disaffected White Youths! I have come from far way through many alien lands to join you!" And all was silent. Until someone threw something. At first I thought somebody was throwing me a big fucking piece of hash. You know, a welcoming gesture. But it was a rock! And then there was another rock, and then another, and they were hitting me, they hurt, they hurt me Sister, and it was like each rock was saying, "Get the hell out goof, we don't want you." They didn't want me! But I know those people. They live on my street! Maybe not exactly my street, but one just like it— and now they're throwing rocks! Like they hated me! Why do they hate me? What did I do to them? What can I do? Where can I go?

LUCY: You're staying with us.

BUSINESSMAN: We want you to stay with us.

BOY: Really?

BUSINESSMAN: I had no right to send you away.

BOY: You didn't?

BUSINESSMAN: You have as much right to this piece of pavement as I do.

BOY: I do?

BUSINESSMAN: You do. *(Sticks hand out.)* Friends again?

BOY: Do we have Marines?

BUSINESSMAN: Yes.

          BUSINESSMAN and BOY shake.

BOY: Because I want them to blow those disaffected bastards off the planet.

          Time passes. BOY falls asleep. The four of them form a perfect tableau, a family portrait.

NUN: He's sleeping.

Engines start in the distance. The three look up.

BUSINESSMAN: Is that engines?

LUCY and the NUN shrug. They all look back down at the BOY.

Do you think he's learned anything?

LUCY: I don't know. But he's certainly lost something.

BUSINESSMAN: We're going to have to watch him like a hawk. Keep food inventory.

NUN: I think I can get through to him.

BUSINESSMAN: We're counting on you.

NUN: I'm sure I can. I just have to find the right words. Leave him to me. You two go back to—to whatever it was you were doing.

LUCY makes a mild protest.

Shoo! Get lost!

LUCY and BUSINESSMAN start to exit, together, as a couple. NUN cradles BOY. Time passes. BOY awakens and NUN begins feeding him.

Listen. I want you to tell me about your family.

BOY says nothing.

You do have a family.

BOY: Yes.

NUN: Well?

BOY: There's nothing to tell. My mother and me live there. My Dad lives over there. My brother lives thataway.

NUN: Do you do things—as a family?

BOY: No.

NUN: OK. Do you do stuff with your neighbours?

BOY: Why?

NUN: For fun. A street barbeque—stuff like that.

            BOY is completely at sea.

            No. Did you ever do anything at school? No. You weren't ever on a team, or the student council? No. Did you ever play in a band?

BOY: Yeah.

NUN: You played in a band. Now we're cooking with gas. And in that band you all had music, right.

BOY: Wrong. Nobody can read it.

NUN: But you had separate parts to play.

BOY: I guess.

NUN: And the separate parts added up to music.

BOY: No. We all play lead guitar. Except for the drummer. He drums. But he quit.

NUN: Oh Lord.

BOY: And the lead vocalist—he sings—he got lost on his way to practice, and ended up in another band. It happens all the time.

NUN: *(Under.)* Oh Lord oh Lord *(Etc.)*

BOY: *(Concerned.)* What's wrong?

            Light up on BUSINESSMAN and LUCY. They are just breaking from a clinch.

BUSINESSMAN: I wish you had asked me. To go home with you.

LUCY: Why.

BUSINESSMAN: I could trust your motives. I can't trust mine. I mean, if I ask, I know why I'm asking, and I hate it. But if you'd asked…

LUCY: I wish I'd been brave enough to ask.

BUSINESSMAN: What is happening to me!? I can't phone, I want him back, I'm paralyzed with you—I'm really feeling paralyzed

LUCY: —With despair?

BUSINESSMAN: Yes.

LUCY: Then let me show you where that leads.

                 LUCY and BUSINESSMAN resume kissing. Light fades on them, and up on NUN. Time passes.

NUN: Do you remember our conversation about your band?

BOY: Yeah. You were really getting fucked sorry up.

NUN: I have another question. In a band, you all play together and, not only that, you play at the same time, right.

BOY: I guess.

NUN: And the result is, you sound better than if you all just went ahead and played separately, right?

BOY: Not with us. We're really bad.

                 NUN groans.

                 No, we're supposed to be bad! That's our appeal! Faster, louder, badder. Actually we never get asked to play.

NUN: Then why the hell do you have a band!?

BOY: So we can get laid. Sorry.

NUN: Quit apologizing to me all the time!

BOY: But you're an (Urban Nun)—

NUN: I don't care if you get laid! I want you to get laid! I want to believe, in fact I pray to the Good Lord that there's a nice—tattooed—babe out there who will ring your flipping chimes.

BOY: You do?

NUN: I want you to be happy! I want the whole fucking world to be happy!

BOY: You swore!

NUN: I'm allowed! I'm the goddamn bride of Christ! *(Pause.)* I need a cigarette. *(Begins an extended patting-down of her body, initially a crossing-self kind of patting, but then clearly a desperate search for cigarettes concealed on her habit.)* Dammit! I'm out!

BOY: *(Also patting himself.)* Me too! Hey—if we could find a bootlegger, we could split a deck.

NUN: *(Pause.)* That's it.

BOY: That's what?

NUN: You've got it!

              Time passes. A lot of time. In fact, autumn arrives and a few leaves fall. Light up on LUCY and BUSINESSMAN. They are clearly lovers. They record together.

LUCY: *(Into tape recorder.)* A man has died and been buried. Confederacies—simple and complex—have formed, up and down, right to the horizon. *(Into the tape recorder, but to BUSINESSMAN.)* And I'm still sitting here dreaming of showers. With you.

BUSINESSMAN: I'm dreaming of a reliable supply of Scotch.

LUCY: White wine for me. Chilled just so.

BUSINESSMAN: I hope this never ends.

LUCY: I hope so too, because when it does, I'll be in the city—and I'll be waiting for you to call me. I'll be wishing I could pick up the phone and call you—but it's not allowed, is it. Eventually, I'll give up. I'll return to the Henry Moores with my recorder. If I was in the city. But I'm not.

BUSINESSMAN: You're here, with me. And I'm paralyzed with despair.

LUCY: So soon? *(Kissing him.)* Show me where that leads.

BUSINESSMAN and LUCY begin making love. Light goes off them. Time is passing—a lot of time again. In fact, it becomes winter. Snowflakes. NUN enters, in winter clothes of a makeshift variety.

NUN: It took me four months to save him. It was the greatest challenge of my life. Well, no. Celibacy's the greatest challenge. But this was a close second. I'm an urban nun. I'd never come face to face with suburban intractability. But I prevailed. The key? Cigarettes. These simple white cylinders transformed a piece of passive disaffection into a constructive member of society, albeit a capitalist. He is no longer Boy. He is a man who deals in smokes. He has been reborn and I call him Lazarus.

BOY appears magically. He has an air of authority.

BOY: Actually, my name's Cody.

NUN: Lazarus Cody.

BOY: As you wish.

BUSINESSMAN: *(Coming on in winter clothes.)* So what's your plan?

LUCY: *(Arriving.)* I've brought the maps.

BOY: We must face the facts. The farmers won't co-operate anymore. The nearest village is three miles away. It's ringed by hostile suburbs full of confusing, curvy streets. Anyway, to even get to the concession road I have to pass through the Bourgeois, Mechanical and Hostile Youths. Plus the Dental Confederation. All of which are charging tolls. And the Dentists have guns. They're hopped up on Novocain. They're firing at anything that looks unflossed. Even if I get past all that, and reach the village—there's no guarantee they'll give us help. They have problems of their own.

BUSINESSMAN: Then what are you suggesting?

BOY: We strike south. *(Pointing.)* That way.

                The others point in the opposite direction.

NUN: That way.

BOY: That way.

LUCY: Too risky. You'd have to cross the tracks.

BOY: I've been timing the trains. There are safe moments.

LUCY: You have too much faith in the predictable. I know a woman who lost both her legs to a random express.

BOY: Fuck. How does she drive? Never mind. We have no choice.

BUSINESSMAN: Lazarus Cody is right. Our food is nearly gone.

LUCY: We're in a tight spot.

BOY: Tomorrow, I'll set out over the tracks. But tonight—we will party.

LUCY is moving off. BUSINESSMAN follows.

NUN: *(To BOY.)* I'm so proud of you.

BOY: Yeah, well, I gotta tell you—it's weird being undisaffected. It gives you a whole different outlook on life. Things begin to look possible. This must be what it's like to be a Marine.

NUN: *(Looking at watch.)* We've got a delivery to make.

BOY: *(Pulling out pad.)* The Bingo Nation. A mile, thataway.

                BOY points one way. NUN indicates opposite direction.

                Really? Man, these straight roads really make me mad. *(Consults pad.)* One case of DuMaurier. Hey— aren't the Bingoites mostly Catholic?

NUN: Affirmative. *(Waving cross.)* We can score some food.

                NUN and BOY exit. Focus on LUCY and BUSINESSMAN.

BUSINESSMAN: What's wrong?

LUCY: I'm worried.

BUSINESSMAN: He seems to know what he's doing.

LUCY: There are so many trains. And we don't know what's on the other side. A lake, a few cottages with tinned food. Some wood he can haul back. Some ice he can fall through. The risks seems so high for such tenuous rewards. And, back here— the hostility is palpable. I hear rumours of fighting down the line—why won't it spread to us? We're small and we have no alliances. *(Pause.)* And I'm pregnant.

BUSINESSMAN: I was wondering when you'd tell me.

LUCY: You guessed?

BUSINESSMAN: I'm a businessman. I know the consequences of merging. Plus: I'm an optimist.

Time passes. A strum from BOY's guitar. The others watch.

BOY: I wrote this for our Union, our small and beleaguered co-op, sandwiched as we are between the Bourgeois Confederacy and the dough-faced Chip-eaters. I call it "The Geography of the Mind".

BUSINESSMAN: That's ambitious.

BOY: I am infected with ambition now. And I owe it to you, all. Here goes nothing.

BOY sings. The tune is an approximation of "Kumbaya".

"My street curves and curves,
My street curves.
My street curves and curves,
My street curves.
My street curves until
It hits the curve
That curves into Northgate Mall."

Applause. NUN exits for cake.

Thanks. I'm working on the next verse. It's something about how Northgate Mall joins up to Westwood Plaza which is across the road from Pinewood Place. Then there's another street just like mine and then things get really ooga-booga because soon you're back on my curving street. The curve being a metaphor.

BUSINESSMAN: Ah—the metaphor.

BOY: Metaphors require no explanation.

LUCY: They are fragile; explanations are not.

BOY: Exactly. Far better to slip the meaning 'neath my
                   listeners' feet, so it's a rug that warms their toes,
                   rather than a squeaky floorboard that trips them.
                   That's another metaphor.

BUSINESSMAN: Save that one.

                   NUN returns, carrying the birthday cake. They
                   sing the Birthday Song to the tune of "Kumbaya".

ALL
BUT BOY: "Happy birthday to you
                   Happy birthday to you..." *(Etc.)*

                   Noise has started under, and BOY has heard it.

BUSINESSMAN: *(Breaking off from song.)* He's not even listening.

LUCY: —He's overwhelmed.

NUN: What's wrong?

BOY: Can you hear something?

                   More noise. This is different from the sound before
                   of the engines starting. This is a rumble, something
                   vaguely menacing, perhaps.

                   Can you hear that?

BUSINESSMAN: Yes.

LUCY: What is it?

BOY: I don't know.

                   BOY has risen above his cake and is looking out.
                   BUSINESSMAN and LUCY look, too. Their arms
                   raise and they point. NUN turns and looks, and
                   there is amazement on her face.

                   Something's changing!

LUCY: Look!

BUSINESSMAN: Look up the road there!

BOY: On the horizon!

They are moving back to their cars.

BUSINESSMAN: What are they yelling?

LUCY: What're they saying up there?

NUN: What's the racket?

BOY: It's moving! They're telling us it's moving! Look ahead—500 yards up.

LUCY: One hundred yards!

BUSINESSMAN: The Bourgeois Confederacy is moving!

BOY: Get in your cars!

LUCY: Start your engines!

BUSINESSMAN: Let's go!

NUN: *(Out, to audience.)* We moved slowly at first. But there was a steadiness to the motion that spoke of something new, of something starting—or ending. And the movement forward was matched by a vaulting in our hearts, an exploding in here like I hadn't felt since I took my Vows, since I walked down that aisle and fell into God's fickle arms.

BOY: *(To LUCY.)* Far out!

LUCY: *(To NUN.)* Hurray!

BUSINESSMAN: We're moving!

They all cheer.

NUN: And I wanted to hug them all, hug my little Union, with whom I'd lived so intimately these past months: the boy who'd turned twenty and been reborn, the woman who'd ceased despairing even before my godchild began growing in her, the man who was finding honesty in her arms... I look over at Lucy and see her smile of resurrecting hope.

LUCY: —A shower, a shower!

NUN: The years of despair are washing off her. And this grin, splitting the face of the father-to-be—

BUSINESSMAN: Scotch!

LUCY: White wine!

BOY: Beer!

NUN: And we drive further and faster, and the dreams fly at us like the winter wind. There's no stopping us now! Nothing is stopping us, we're moving forward, we're moving fast now, faster now, faster. And I want to tell them how much I love them all.

                They aren't parallel anymore.

                But...

BUSINESSMAN: Lucy?

NUN: We aren't staying parallel! Lucy's a length ahead!

BUSINESSMAN: Lucy!

NUN: You can barely see the look of fear when she turns and—

LUCY: Where are you!?

NUN: And now she's three lengths ahead, speeding with the remnants of the Bourgeois Confederacy!

BOY: HEY!

BUSINESSMAN: Jesus! *(To BOY.)* Hurry!

BOY: Wait up!

NUN: But he's falling back! He's falling back with the Chip-eaters!

BOY: Faster!

NUN: We're splitting apart!

LUCY: Where are you!

NUN: And we are racing now, racing to the city and our group has dissolved a thousand times more easily than it formed; it's dissipating amid the roaring engines and our surprised cries. And my heart pounds so hard and each pound hurts more than the one before—I know it's over, it's really over...

> *BOY has put on the BUSINESSMAN's headphones.*

There'll be no more forays down the line threatening up food. No more lovemaking in the car beside me, no more litter or curses from the boy I love, none of the things that have brought me such joy.

> *BUSINESSMAN is on his phone again.*

And you want it to start again, you wish this could stop, you want to go back to how it was

> *LUCY has begun murmuring into her Dictaphone.*

Except we're hurtling—

Hurtling—

At a thousand miles an hour

Towards lights that dazzle

That dazzle.

That blind.

And I don't understand this urge;

I don't understand this race

Among faceless cars

On nameless roads

Where no one knows anything

Anymore

About the others.

Where we only crave isolation

From each other.

Where everyone looks dead—

Ahead.

Where we only look straight—

Ahead.

And I have to ask

I have to ask this

I have to ask you

Who does all this serve?

Who's really gaining?

Who's really losing?

Why are we doing it?

Why are we doing this ourselves?

Does anyone know?

> *Sound out.*

> *Black.*

The End